How Documentaries Work

T0398872

How Documentaries Work

Jacob Bricca, ACE

OXFORD
UNIVERSITY PRESS

OXFORD
UNIVERSITY PRESS

Oxford University Press is a department of the University of Oxford. It furthers
the University's objective of excellence in research, scholarship, and education
by publishing worldwide. Oxford is a registered trade mark of Oxford University
Press in the UK and certain other countries.

Published in the United States of America by Oxford University Press
198 Madison Avenue, New York, NY 10016, United States of America.

© Oxford University Press 2023

Library of Congress Cataloging-in-Publication Data
Names: Bricca, Jacob, author.
Title: How documentaries work / by Jacob Bricca.
Description: New York, NY : Oxford University Press, [2023] |
Includes bibliographical references.
Identifiers: LCCN 2022029907 (print) | LCCN 2022029908 (ebook) |
ISBN 9780197554104 (hardback) | ISBN 9780197554111 (paperback) |
ISBN 9780197554135 (epub)
Subjects: LCSH: Documentary films—Production and direction.
Classification: LCC PN1995.9.D6 B747 2022 (print) | LCC PN1995.9.D6
(ebook) | DDC 070.1/8—dc23/eng/20220913
LC record available at https://lccn.loc.gov/2022029907
LC ebook record available at https://lccn.loc.gov/2022029908

DOI: 10.1093/oso/9780197554104.001.0001

Contents

Introduction

Deconstructing the Documentary

In conducting research for my book *Documentary Editing: Principles and Practice,* I interviewed fellow documentary editors to gather their insights into the process of cutting a documentary. As I sat down to turn their stories into words on the page, I was struck by an exciting but uncomfortable feeling: I was revealing secrets. There are numerous skills one utilizes in crafting a documentary, and many of them are unknown to the audiences that ultimately consume them. Some of these are tiny little elisions, but others are more substantial—and possibly more questionable. As I chatted with a director I had worked for and asked permission to share the details of a scene that I had cut for him, he chuckled mirthfully. "Oh, Jacob, you're going to give away all our secrets!" He was joking, of course. But the very fact that I felt the need to ask permission was testament to the fact that there is something tricky going on in the production of nonfiction material.

When Norman Hirschy at Oxford University Press approached me about writing this book, I knew that a similar truth-telling would be necessary. There exists today a large gulf between the conversations that documentary filmmakers have among themselves about what they produce and the understanding that most viewers have about what they see onscreen. This is not to say that viewers are incapable of discernment or that they accept what is given to them at face value; to the contrary, most are highly sophisticated and do the work of reading documentary codes with extraordinary skill. But the codes themselves—the patterned execution of documentary

How Documentaries Work. Jacob Bricca, Oxford University Press. © Oxford University Press 2023.
DOI: 10.1093/oso/9780197554104.003.0001

tropes and conventions—need examination if audiences are to fully understand what they are consuming. Few are the filmmakers that have time, budget, or inclination to follow Penny Lane's example of building an exhaustive online appendix to her documentary *Nuts!*, which dissects the film passage by passage and characterizes each one with labels like "Tricky Edit," "Chronological Distortion," and "Probable Invention." Without such documentation, viewers are left to their own devices.

Meanwhile, documentarians have been boldly pushing the medium forward with highly stylized reenactments, staged events, and provocative intermingling of traditional documentary elements with those previously reserved for fiction. As documentary has recently come into its own as an auteur's medium, it has also lost some of its distance from scripted fiction, which begs the question: How should we read documentaries? If, according to the late author and documentary editor Dai Vaughan, "To read a film as fiction . . . implies that everything . . . is subject to authorial control,"[1] then how, exactly, do we read a documentary, which is supposedly about the untamed, uncontrollable real world and therefore beyond such control? How should we interpret was we see?

* * *

"Tiger at the Bronx Zoo Tests Positive for Coronavirus," states the headline on a story dated April 5, 2020, on the CNET website (Figure I.1). Looking at the story, one's eye is immediately drawn to the picture of the tiger as it roams the grounds of the Bronx Zoo, and one may also note that it is one of "seven big cats at the zoo that are showing symptoms." The picture caption identifies it as "a 4-year-old tiger at the Bronx Zoo." This all seems rather unremarkable.

Yet a look at the photo credit reveals a piece of interesting information: the source of the picture is listed as "James Deverney / Getty." A quick web search reveals that the photo is for sale from Getty Images, one of the largest stock image archives in the world (Figure I.2).

Looking at the details on the Getty site, we can now confirm that while this picture was indeed taken at the Bronx Zoo, it was done so

Tiger at the Bronx Zoo tests positive for coronavirus

Seven big cats at the zoo are showing symptoms of COVID-19.

Jackson Ryan ☺ April 5, 2020 2:34 p.m. PT   ES ↷ 💬 ⑤   (▶ LISTEN · 02:00)

A 4-year-old tiger at the Bronx Zoo in New York has tested positive for COVID-19
James Devaney/Getty

A 4-year-old tiger at the Bronx Zoo in New York has tested positive for COVID-19, the disease caused by the coronavirus, according to a statement by the Wildlife Conservation Society. Three more tigers and three lions have developed a dry cough

Figure I.1 A news story on CNET.com

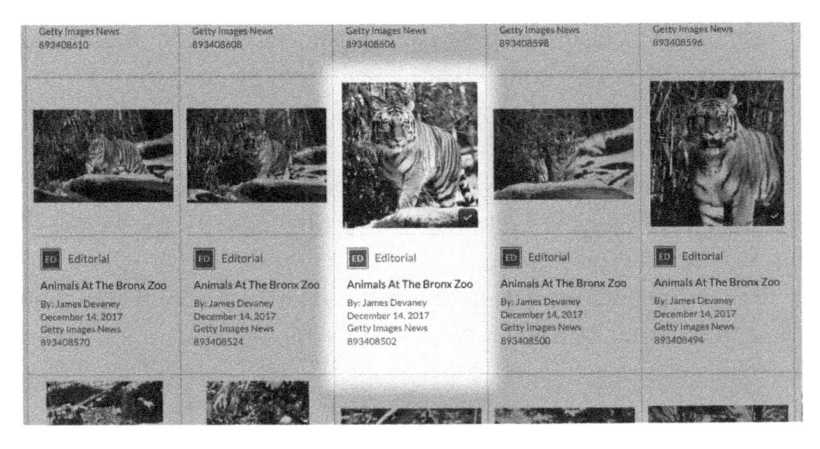

Figure I.2 Photo for sale on the Getty Images website

in December 2017, not April 2020 when the story was written. This means that a four-year-old tiger in the Bronx Zoo has indeed tested positive for the virus, but it's unlikely that this is the tiger in question or that the one in the picture is four years old.

Let's note that none of the individual elements carry any false claims. But it's precisely in the implied relationship between all of these true things that we find ambiguity and slippage. Seeing the words "a 4-year-old tiger" directly under the picture created an impression—*here's the tiger that the article talks about*—that is not fully accurate. We are instead looking at an impression of the real thing, a serviceable facsimile.

This loose relationship between what images seem to represent and what they actually depict is fundamental to documentary film-making. In fact, it is the very indeterminacy of an image's origin that makes many common techniques of documentary storytelling possible. At one crucial moment in Asif Kapadia's 2019 film *Diego Maradona*, a documentary about the world-famous Argentinian footballer, Maradona's ex-girlfriend Cristiana Sinagra speculates in an old television interview about why he refuses to acknowledge paternity of their son. Painting a complex psychological portrait of the emotional toll his lies are taking on him, she says with pity, "I think he suffers for this." Precisely at this moment, the audience sees Maradona in slow motion, taking the field for a match in front of tens of thousands of cheering fans, with a stark look on his face (Figure I.3). Upon the utterance of the word "suffers," Maradona grimaces, as if thinking about something particularly painful. Precisely what was on Maradona's mind at that particular moment in a crowded stadium over thirty years ago is unknowable, but it could have been anything from a tight hamstring to pregame jitters. In the logic of the film, however, he is feeling the crushing weight of his own moral shortcomings.

Perhaps no one summed up this concept more succinctly than the aforementioned Dai Vaughan.

> The documentary response is one in which the image is perceived as signifying what it appears to record; a documentary film is one which

I think he suffers for this.

Figure I.3 Diego Maradona suffers in *Diego Maradona*

seeks, by whatever means, to elicit this response; and the documentary movement is the history of the strategies which have been adopted to this end.

Documentary will be consequent upon what it appears to show, rather than upon what it necessarily does show; and the relationship between the two is a matter for the filmmakers' ethics, inaccessible to the viewer. Yet the assumptions which the viewer makes about this relationship, on the basis of signals intended or unintended, will inform his perception of the film. To make a documentary is therefore to persuade the viewer that what appears to be is.[2]

* * *

Moving pictures are fictions. When we sit in a movie theater or in front of a laptop screen, we are not actually watching anything move. A series of still frames are being shown in rapid succession, fooling our brain into seeing movement and working in tandem with a set of perceptual cues that allow us to decode two-dimensional images as three-dimensional space. If the film is compelling, we react just as though something were actually happening—we laugh, we cry, we are scared, we are moved. Just as our brain experiences dreams as if they are real while they are occurring, a powerful movie produces convincing sensory stimulation that simulates lived experience.

This comes as a surprise to no one, yet its implications are profound. It means that when we watch a movie or a television show we are entering a dream space that doesn't actually exist anywhere but inside our own minds. When the content is a scripted, fictional film, we give implicit acknowledgment to this fact—we know it isn't real. But when we watch a documentary, a much more complex and problematic dynamic is in play because we relate these experiences back to the historical reality that we all share. It seems all *too* real. As filmmaker and sociologist Edgar Morin said prophetically in 1960,

> We ought to know that fiction film is by definition much less illusory and much less deceitful than so-called documentary cinema, because both director and spectator know that it's fiction, which is to say that its truth is conveyed through the imagination. On the other hand, documentary cinema hides its fiction and its imaginings behind the facade of reality.[3]

While documentaries may seem to be fundamentally distinct from fiction films, in fact they carry far more similarities than differences. "All films are documentaries," stated Bill Nichols provocatively in 2001 in the first edition of his seminal book *Introduction to Documentary*.[4] As he pointed out, both types of films are created by placing cameras in front of human persons at various moments in time and constitute a record of those moments. While the moments in a fiction film were staged, the moments did exist, or, as Vaughan helpfully puts it, "Any fiction film can be perceived as a documentary on its own making."[5] Whether they involve actors delivering lines from a script or real people performing as themselves, all films are christened with moments of human performance captured by a camera.[6]

Nichols goes on to point out the similarities between professional actors and documentary participants. Film actors are trained to ignore the highly unnatural environment of a film set, on which film lights, props, and scenery are piled high around them and a dozen crew members watch their every move. Directors of documentaries often look for a similar lack of self-consciousness when they are researching their projects and may drop subjects from the production whose response is to freeze up in front of the camera. But which is the more authentic response: to acknowledge the artificiality of the situation and wonder about the consequences of the shoot, or to pretend the camera and the consequences aren't there?

Perhaps that's a false dichotomy. Documentarian Jean Rouch claimed that "when people are being recorded, the reactions that they have are always infinitely more sincere than those they have when they are not being recorded."[7] Frederick Wiseman agreed, claiming that "most people aren't *capable* of changing their behavior on camera. It takes a great actor to be able to do that, but most of us don't have the skills." Or maybe the most authentic documentary is one that highlights its own duality, like the Robert Greene film *Actress*, which simultaneously plays out as a documentary about actress Brandy Burre's midlife career crisis and one about Burre playing a role in a documentary about the same thing (Figure I.4). (Slumped over a beanbag in her kids' playroom, she says, "I'm not

Figure I.4 Brandy Burre plays herself in *Actress*

acting, so this is my creative outlet, I guess," before stopping and re-peating the exact same lines, as if trying to get the halfhearted sentiment just right for the camera.) And what are we to think of the highly refined storytelling conventions that are operative in so many documentaries that require the arrangement of reality into formulaic models of exposition, development, and payoff?

It again begs the question: what *is* a documentary? Scottish filmmaker John Grierson's 1926 definition as a film that practices "the creative treatment of actuality" is pithy, but policing its boundaries has always been a fraught endeavor.[8] Author Michael Rabiger tries to separate documentaries from propaganda by asking whether the filmmaker begins the process with the point already firmly established (propaganda) or from a position of honest inquiry (documentary).[9] Yet the proliferation of sponsored documentaries leaves some films in limbo, like the 2018 documentary *Breaking2*, sponsored by Nike. The production is really an extended, multipart Nike commercial, since its products are in nearly every frame and many of the protagonists are the company's employees, but it would be unhelpful to ignore the fact that it strongly follows standard documentary conventions.[10] What about hybrid films like Alfonso Ruizpalacios's *Una Película de Policías* (*A Cop Movie*), which has a segment showing two actors going through real-life police academy training in order to more faithfully perform their parts in the reenactments that take up most of the running time of the film, or *American Animals*, which features documentary interviews with the perpetrators of a bungled art heist in 2004 but consists mostly of reenacted scenes? The nonscripted portions of each of these films are tiny, but don't the films differ only in quantitative terms (rather than qualitative ones) from any other documentary that utilizes reenactments?[11] What about reality shows like *The Bachelor*? They break the very first rule that most documentarians hold sacred—the idea that the documented event is separate from (and exists without prior connection to) the film. Yet numerous are the films in which documentarians conspire to create events expressly for the purpose of filming them (*Icarus, Forks over Knives, Jackass Forever*). And it's important to note that the storytelling strategies practiced in traditional feature documentaries and docuseries are not fundamentally different from those at play on television shows like *Love Island* or *The Great British Baking Show*.

In my research for this book I talked to directors, producers, and craft persons of all kinds; I also scoured my own career as a documentary producer, director, and editor for useful anecdotes. I made the choice to define documentary broadly. While this volume concentrates on feature-length films and docuseries, to exclude discussion of reality television and other unscripted shows would do a disservice to our goal of elucidating the structural conventions and commonplace practices of the form, so these genres are included as well. Indeed, anything that illuminates what is usually taken for granted is fair game, for it is often what is taken for granted that is the most in need of dissection.

I see this book as an opportunity to build a bridge between practitioners and viewers and to open a discussion about how meaning in documentaries is made. That discussion is already in progress, but while robust debates occur at conferences like "Getting Real" (sponsored by the International Documentary Association), the Flaherty Seminar (sponsored by International Film Seminars, Inc.), and "Visible Evidence" (put on by the academics who make up the Visible Evidence Governing Council), they attract mainly practitioners and academics, and much of the discourse in documentary studies is understandably focused on highly specific theoretical issues rather than holistic analysis. A big-picture view on documentary is needed now more than ever, for as we head into the heart of the 2020s, documentary is increasingly popular, increasingly alive with creativity, and also increasingly beset with ethical conundrums. While this book is not written primarily as a forum for addressing those conundrums (readers would be well advised to pick up a copy of Bill Nichols's *Introduction to Documentary*), it does attempt to lay bare some of the practices that bring them to the fore. By reading this book I hope to give the reader the tools to decipher, decode, and deconstruct the complex flows of information in a documentary.

Notes

1. Dai Vaughan, *For Documentary* (Berkeley: University of California Press, 1999), 130.
2. Vaughan, *For Documentary*, 59.
3. Edgar Morin, "Chronicle of a Film," in *Cine-Ethnography*, ed. Steven Feld (Minneapolis: University of Minnesota Press, 2003), 229–65.
4. Bill Nichols, *Introduction to Documentary*, 1st ed. (Bloomington: Indiana University Press, 2001), 36.
5. Vaughan, *For Documentary*, 58.
6. Animated films and those with heavy use of computer graphics complicate this statement with respect to fiction films.
7. James Blue, "The Films of Jean Rouch," *Film Comment* 4, nos. 2–3 (Fall–Winter 1967): 84–86.
8. Laura Marcus, "'The Creative Treatment of Actuality': John Grierson, Documentary Cinema and 'Fact' in the 1930s," in *Intermodernism: Literary Culture in Mid-Twentieth-Century Britain*, ed. Kristin Bluemel (Edinburgh: Edinburgh University Press, 2009), 190.
9. Michael Rabiger, *Directing the Documentary*, 6th ed. (New York: Focal Press, 2015), 22.
10. "The State of Journalism on the Documentary Filmmaking Scene," published by the Center for Media & Social Impact in September 2021, lists some recent examples of undisclosed conflicts of interest in recent documentaries. https://cmsimpact.org/report/the-state-of-journalism-on-the-documentary-filmmaking-scene/p/documentary-film-growing-faster-than-its-standards/.
11. To be precise, interviews take up 11.4 minutes out of the total running time of 117 minutes of the film.

1
Raw Materials

Documentary films are collages. Any single passage of a documentary is apt to contain material from a huge variety of sources, so it's useful for us to begin by breaking them down into their constituent parts. Documentaries vary greatly in style and content, but they all consist of some combination of verité footage, interviews, archival materials, reenactments and animations, title cards, music, and voice-over narration. Each element represents a different kind of intervention in the real world, and each speaks to the audience in its own way.

Verité

In a scene from *The Bad Kids*, the 2016 Sundance Special Jury Prize Winner that I edited with Mary Lampson, Joey, a smart but troubled teen, arrives back at Black Rock High School in Joshua Tree, California, after several weeks of truancy.[1] "I miss my coffee pot; I miss my coffee grind; I miss everything about my house," says Joey as he takes a seat at a table next to a friend, where they have been assigned the duty of cutting out photos for a display case featuring the school's next graduating class (Figure 1.1). "Why'd you leave?" his friend asks, mirroring the audience's own curiosity about his situation. "My mom, she accused me of stealing somebody's drugs. I woke up to her screaming and yelling at me," Joey says ruefully. "It's nothing new . . . she was on another bad trip. I walked out the door." The poignancy and sadness of the scene is palpable: here Joey sits,

How Documentaries Work. Jacob Bricca, Oxford University Press. © Oxford University Press 2023.
DOI: 10.1093/oso/9780197554104.003.0002

Figure 1.1   Joey cuts out graduation pictures in *The Bad Kids*

cutting out pictures of other students who will be graduating while he, because of his poor attendance, has hardly moved the needle on the requirements for graduation.

For a filmmaker seeking to reproduce many of the storytelling conventions of traditional Hollywood films, verité is the ticket.[2] Here a documentarian brings the camera directly into the lives of the protagonists. The similarity to scripted fiction is unmistakable: the audience witnesses things *through the interactions of the characters with each other and the world around them.* Instead of telling the audience about his situation in an interview, Joey relates everything to another character, providing pitch-perfect exposition. A documentary shooter will often "cover" a scene in a way that facilitates the editing, getting an establishing shot to identify the location, shooting wide shots to communicate the geography of the participants, and catching moments of compelling drama in medium shots and close-ups. Crucially, exposition and subtext can be expressed directly through character action, something that every screenwriting manual labors to endorse.

It is crucial to point out that verité scenes are an imaginary experience created for the viewer. In the scene from *The Bad Kids*, for instance, the dialogue has been extensively rearranged to feature this one succinct exchange and makes it seem as though Joey started talking about his departure from home as soon as he sat down. Indeed, while the camera rolled for well over thirty minutes, the final scene clocks in at a mere thirty-three seconds. As we will see in Chapter 6, with every cut something has been excised.

Interviews

When many people think of documentaries, one of the signature elements that comes to mind is the interview. Instead of putting the audience directly into a situation with verité, interviews allow the filmmaker to tell the audience a story or relate an observation through the account of a participant, observer, or expert. Here the audience is one step removed from the action, for instead of *witnessing* things play out, they are *hearing someone explain in words* how they played out, or how the person feels about them. A picture is painted for the audience, but as *description* and *summary* rather than as seemingly direct experience.

The words spoken in an interview are important, but an interviewee's body language and tone of voice carry another rich layer of information. A subtle vocal inflection can turn the meaning of a statement into its opposite with just a hint of sarcasm. What's more, every interview is an opportunity to invite subjects to ponder the event in question as they speak. As editor Jason Rosenfield, ACE notes, "[The subject] may be giving a description of a past event, but it becomes something in the present because they are reliving an experience in their mind and having an emotional reaction all over again. In a sense you're able to watch what it was like to be there, even though you're only listening to somebody talk."

The interview is a strongly interventionist move. Whereas in verité the filmmaker only learns what participants are thinking if they happen to speak about it to others, here the filmmaker can pry it right out of them. Steve James, director of *Hoop Dreams, The Interrupters,* and *America to Me,* is well aware of the difference and chooses to include interviews in his films.

It's rare for me to see a pure verité film that really gets into all the dimensions of what's going on in a way that's satisfying to me as a viewer. I want to know more about the people, I want to know more about what they're thinking, I want to know more about what's led to this moment. A pure verité filmmaker is captive to some degree to what they're able to capture, and I don't like being captive to that because it can just reinforce stereotypes. If you do a pure verité film about poor people in the inner city, so much of their lives, purely observed, can seem to reinforce certain stereotypes about those communities. But if you talk to them and you start to really get inside them with interviews, then those scenes that could reinforce stereotypes suddenly don't do that anymore. I also find that people have tremendous abilities to analyze and reflect on their own lives. I want people who watch my films to think of the people *in* the films as not just subjects for scrutiny and empathy, but also as sources of true insight.

Archival

Put simply, archival material is material that predates the making of the film. Archival documents include home movie recordings, digital and print photos, segments of old films, television news programs and commercials, written documents (old letters as well as digital files), and audio recordings.

The use of archival material in documentaries is as varied as documentaries themselves. It can be the subject of the film itself, as in essay documentaries like Thom Anderson's *Los Angeles Plays Itself*, Irene Lusztig's *The Motherhood Archives*, or Jayne Loader, Kevin Rafferty, and Pierce Rafferty's *The Atomic Cafe*, in which the clever arrangement of clips from 1950s government propaganda films reveals the alarming misinformation about nuclear fallout that they contained. The clips may come with lower-third title cards providing full attribution of the source (as in the first example) or with none at all (as in the other two), depending on the whims of the director. They may be selectively employed to illustrate an idea put forth in interviews, serving as the visual confirmation for an assertion made with words. Or they can simply be used to "set the scene" of an event that takes place in the past, as when driving shots of Hollywood Boulevard and Sunset Boulevard are used to bring the audience into the world of the 1970s Los Angeles for many scenes in *Be Water*, the ESPN documentary on the kung fu movie star and filmmaking pioneer Bruce Lee. Here the archival footage is useful for its essential banality and *lack* of connection to another narrative; whether it was taken from a stock footage library or an establishing shot from a fiction film, its meaning here is simply: *Los Angeles, mid-1970s.*

Because its only defining characteristic is that it predates the making of the film, "archival" is a large, malleable category with seemingly endless functions. It also tends to carry a powerful and seductive aura of authenticity, which we will discuss in detail in Chapter 10.

Reenactments and Animation

Reenactments are often employed by filmmakers to solve a fundamental problem: some portion of the story took place before they arrived to document it, or access to the locations where it took place was impossible (prisons, hospitals, etc.). There is no chance of capturing these moments in verité, and while interviews can *tell* the audience about what happened (past tense) they cannot put the audience directly "in the moment" to experience it for themselves. If there are no suitable archival materials, filmmakers are left with two primary options: reenactments or animations.[3]

The use of reenactments is as old as motion pictures themselves, and it is fitting that *Nanook of the North*, commonly thought of as the first feature documentary, used them liberally. Robert Flaherty's intimate depiction of life among a small group of Inuit in northern Quebec showed "Nanook" (not his real name) acting out fishing and hunting practices that were already a relic of an earlier age.[4] As Bill Nichols remarked, "[Flaherty's] entire salvage anthropology model of coaxing Allakariallak to do what 'Nanook' would have done some thirty years earlier, without motorized vehicles, rifles, canned food, wood-frame homes, or filmmakers along for the ride, amounted to one colossal, unacknowledged reenactment and, therefore, fraud."[5] The operative word here is *unacknowledged*. If the audience is unaware of what they're watching, the justification for the proposition starts to unravel. This is the key distinction made in the codes of ethics put forward by major journalist organizations, such as this one from a consortium of journalist organizations that includes the Society of Professional Journalists and the Association of Black Journalists:

> Avoid misleading reenactments or staged news events. If reenactment is necessary to tell a story, label it.[6]

Back in the 1980s when newsmagazines like *A Current Affair* and *Hard Copy* covered true crime stories in a tabloid style, they would do just that, putting a large "Reenactment" title card over the first shot of a reenactment segment, or sometimes over the entire scene. As this journalism-based true crime trend crossed over into prime time in the late 1980s, these explicitly labeled reenactment segments had a short life on shows like *Saturday Night with Connie Chung* (later renamed *Face to Face with Connie Chung*) and NBC's *Yesterday, Today, and Tomorrow*. The latter featured anchor Mary Alice Williams explaining the rules of engagement on the first show of the series: "In some cases we will faithfully recreate events, carefully documenting every important detail and always clearly identifying every re-creation; scenes and stories not identified as re-creations are real."[7] Yet these shows received cool receptions from critics who saw them as demeaning to the hard-news focus of the storied news departments of the networks that they played on, and with scant interest from audiences they quickly died out.[8]

Meanwhile, documentaries made outside of the major news organizations and their strict labeling guidelines took a different approach, signaling the presence of a reenactment through purely formal means. Reenactments today will often gesture self-consciously to their own artificiality, with actors representing key characters shown from disadvantaged, oblique angles. Their faces are not shown and, as a rule, they do not speak.[9] Whereas scenes in a fiction film are staged *toward* the audience so that the spectator has an easy view of the action, in reenactments the action is usually staged *away*. The shots often feel furtive, just a bit voyeuristic, giving the audience an intentionally partial view. The images are gestural in nature, hinting at a larger world that is never shown, but which can be imagined by the audience. Sometimes it's the color grading or lighting setup that will set a reenactment apart, or there will be some other way of distinguishing them from the other material. In The Jinx, for instance, nearly all archival elements appear with a soft-edged border around them, while reenactments are shown full screen.

These coded formal gestures allow documentary filmmakers to feel that they are being transparent with the audience about the source of the footage while avoiding an ugly "Reenactment" title card. This, of course, assumes that the audience can read the code. As we will discuss in the concluding chapter of this book, the gestures used these days by some nonfiction filmmakers are becoming so subtle as to be almost impossible to detect.

Solving issues of access is not the only reason that documentarians utilize reenactments. Ever since Errol Morris boldly used the aesthetics of film noir to inform the deliberately stylized and spare reenactments he created for his 1988 documentary *The Thin Blue Line*, fellow documentarians have seen the potential of using reenactments to bring a unique visual style to their films. Even more recently, Joshua Oppenheimer utilized the staging of reenactments as a central way of exploring the point of view of his subjects in *The Act of Killing*, allowing the perpetrators of genocidal crimes to reenact their own brutal torture and killings as a way of exploring the psychology of evil. Other filmmakers such as Trinh T. Minh-ha and Sarah Polley have played with the ability of deliberately staged scenes to explore issues of truth and selfhood.

Reenactment has been memorably accomplished via animation in recent years, sometimes in concert with the need to obscure the identities of those involved, as in Jonas Poher Rasmussen's *Flee*, which tells the story of an Afghani refugee known as Amin. Here the level of abstraction is one step greater than in live-action reenactments, as the visual world of the film extends to environments that may have no direct referent in the real world. As with any other documentary element, tone and style vary widely, from the desaturated watercolors portraying scenes of torture in Rania Elmalky's harrowing *489 Days* to the deliberately cartoonish drawings of copulating goats in Penny Lane's comedic *Nuts!* Reenactment meets animation in an even more literal way in Keith Maitland's *Tower*, which uses live-action reenactments as the raw material for the rotoscoped, animated images of a 1966 mass shooting on the University of Texas campus and manages to bring the audience into a visual space that is at once safely removed from the horrors of the account and also highly emotional in its own way. And when documentarians employ animated infographics, they can give a visceral, embodied feel to abstract concepts and ideas, as in the investigative documentary *The Bleeding Edge* when the comparison is made between the large clinical trials needed for drug approval versus the lax requirements for approval of medical devices (see Figure 1.2). The visceral experience of seeing just a few animated figures on one side and a whole crowd of them on the other hammers the point home.

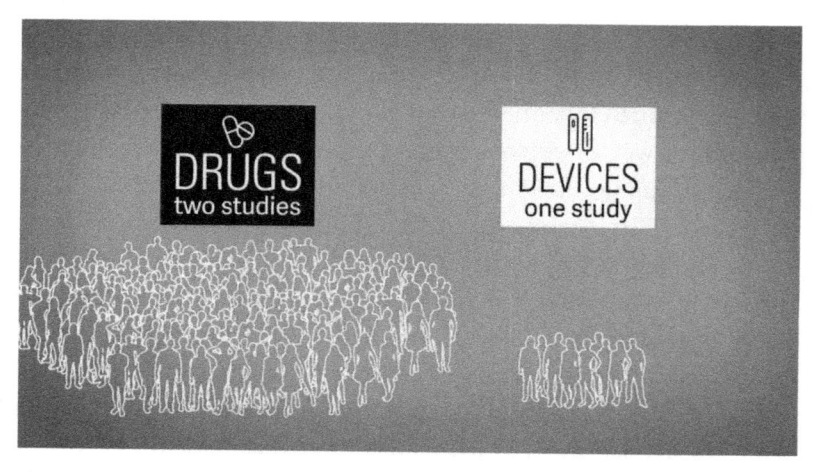

Figure 1.2 An animated graphic from *The Bleeding Edge*

Voice-over Narration

If you've ever seen a Ken Burns documentary, you are familiar with this mode of address. In his direct, authoritative voice, Peter Coyote utters the following words as the eight-part series *Country Music* begins:

> Country music rose from the bottom up, from the songs Americans sang to themselves in farm fields and railroad yards to ease them through their labors, and songs they sang to each other on the porches and in the parlors of their homes when the day's work was done.

When you come upon a narrated portion of a documentary, the filmmaker has abandoned all pretense of having the story tell itself, and instead is going to tell it to the audience directly. If the narrator assumes the traditional "voice of God" (i.e., the speaker plays no other role in the film and is not otherwise referenced), it claims a great deal of authority. The voice is faceless and omniscient and operates with the unspoken assumption that definitive answers to difficult questions do indeed exist. *Facts are facts*, this kind of narration implies. *We're just telling it like it is.* Audiences may evaluate such claims based in part on the reputation of the show. A program on *Frontline*, the PBS investigative news documentary show that has been running since 1983, has a certain cachet simply because it's *Frontline*—it has a solid reputation and is known to have high journalistic standards. Another film may build up its authority through the credentials of the experts that populate its interviews or the past credits of the individuals listed as producers and executive producers.

The identity of the narrator may help establish this authority, and the celebrity narrator is a common choice of many documentaries fortunate enough to have the connections to cast one. This is a relatively low-level commitment on the part of the talent (who can often record the entire narration for a documentary in a single afternoon) but for filmmakers it can bring a whole new level of marketing potential to their product. Certain pairings may seem arbitrary—what did Nicole Kidman actually know about the Lost Boys of Sudan when she voiced the narration for *God Grew Tired of Us*, and what does Pierce Brosnan know about *Hope in the Time of AIDS?*—but other pairings are more apt. Leonardo DiCaprio is known to be a climate activist; therefore his involvement with *The 11th Hour, Ice on Fire,* and *Before the Flood* seems to make sense. Danny Glover is a lifelong social justice activist; therefore his involvement as narrator of *James Baldwin: Witness* has a superficially natural fit.[10] And a few actors become known precisely because of their talent for narrating documentaries, which becomes a self-reinforcing phenomenon. The king of American documentary narration is surely the aforementioned Peter Coyote, whose website boasts an astonishing 175 films that he has narrated. This parade of mostly male names is indicative of the unfortunate fact that in many quarters the male voice is still considered authoritative in a way the female voice is not. Centuries of ingrained stereotypes put male voices in sync with adjectives like "disinterested" and "factual" and female voices as "evocative" or even "suggestive." Another way to put it: a male voice is seen as a "neutral" choice, whereas a female voice is sometimes felt to carry some additional connotation.

This traditional role of the narrator—a voice outside the film, speaking omnisciently about events that occur inside of it—changes significantly when the voice speaking is someone who has a role to play within the film. Filmmaker Michael Moore's upbringing in Flint, Michigan, is crucial to his origin story as depicted in many of his documentaries (*Roger & Me, Fahrenheit 9/11, Capitalism: A Love Story*), and Judith Helfand's battle with cervical cancer at age twenty-five is a crucial piece of backstory for the first-person environmental narrative in *Blue Vinyl.*

But regardless of the voice's relationship to the events portrayed in the film, it nonetheless is about *telling* the audience something rather than showing it to them. From the filmmaker's point of view its function is often to sew up holes and stitch together relationships between aspects of the film that would otherwise be unwieldy to explain. It provides a summarizing/bonding function, shifting focus or bringing one aspect of the film into relationship with another. We will continue to explore the use of voice-over narration in Chapter 2 as we interrogate its precise, moment-to-moment interaction with pictures, and again in Chapter 4 when we consider its relationship to the presence or absence of the filmmaker.

Title Cards

Many documentary filmmakers are wary of using narration. "I think my main feeling about film [is that it] should not lecture," said D. A. Pennebaker in 1961,[11] reflecting a sentiment that would guide the *direct cinema* and *cinema verité* documentary movements of the 1960s. Anything that smacked of a heavy-handed "voice of authority" became suspect, and this sentiment has continued to carry weight in the decades since. Yet for many filmmakers, the functions served by narration—neatly summarizing crucial nuggets of information, bridging the gaps between unrelated scenes—are crucial to their storytelling, so an alternative way of achieving a similar goal is the title card. The voice of the film is still registered, but instead of an actual human voice speaking to the audience, the words are printed on the screen for the audience to apprehend on their own. Now the film seems to be giving the audience more agency and more breathing room; they are allowed to read the text at their own pace and in their own inner voice rather than in one chosen by the film.

Yet despite the patina of neutrality with a white-on-black title, tonal shading is still very much in play. The pocket of space taken up by the title card is precisely timed and carefully calibrated to reflect urgency or languidness. Font choice can give off a playful vibe or a stark one. And the precise language used is carefully thought out: Does the text speak in the language of everyday life, or does it phrase things as a textbook might, with an aura of settled fact? Does it speak in a disinterested way, or is it embodied as the idiosyncratic voice of the filmmaker, as in the opening lines of text in *Hale County This Morning, This Evening*, shot in black communities in Alabama.

> The discovering began after I moved to Alabama
> in 2009 to teach photography and coach basketball
>
> Photographing in my day-to-day I began filming,
> using time to figure out how we've come to be seen

Here both the filmmaker's presence and his intention are announced. The language is both poetic and subjective, and declares that it will be about discovering and countering stereotypes about African Americans. Elsewhere, even when it's being used to deliver a crucial piece of information—many residents here work at the nearby catfish plant—it does so in a poetic voice that speaks of local knowledge, personal connection with the participants, and a comfort with colloquialisms:

> Near everybody works at a catfish plant
> Quincy does it, Daniel dreads it
> After twenty years, Mary could cough a catfish

Contrast this with the starkly dramatic opening to the 2007 film *Outrage*, which has shades of Edward R. Murrow (see Figures 1.3–1.5). Or compare it to the dry "just the facts" orientation of *Fire at Sea* (see Figures 1.6–1.10).

We will have more to say about title cards in Chapter 7.

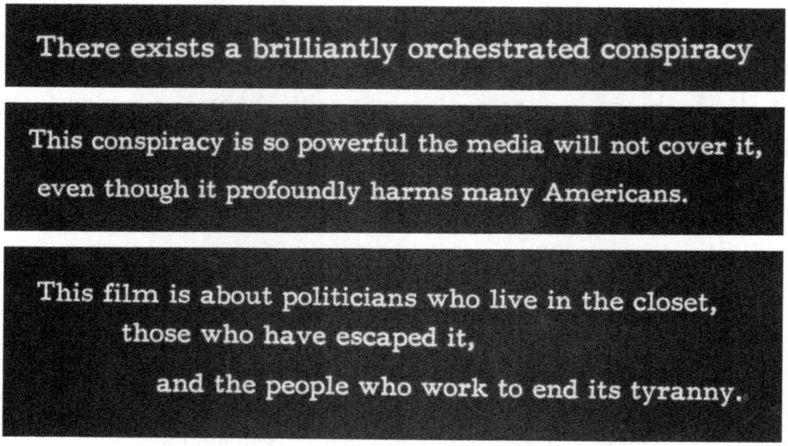

There exists a brilliantly orchestrated conspiracy

This conspiracy is so powerful the media will not cover it, even though it profoundly harms many Americans.

This film is about politicians who live in the closet, those who have escaped it, and the people who work to end its tyranny.

Figures 1.3–1.5 The opening titles from *Outrage*

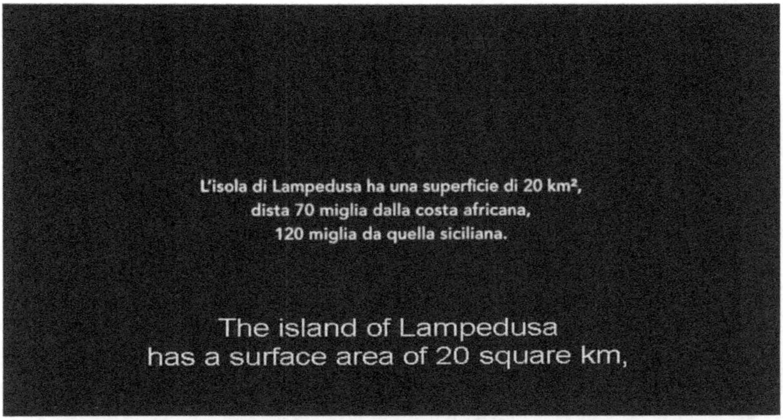

L'isola di Lampedusa ha una superficie di 20 km²,
dista 70 miglia dalla costa africana,
120 miglia da quella siciliana.

The island of Lampedusa
has a surface area of 20 square km,

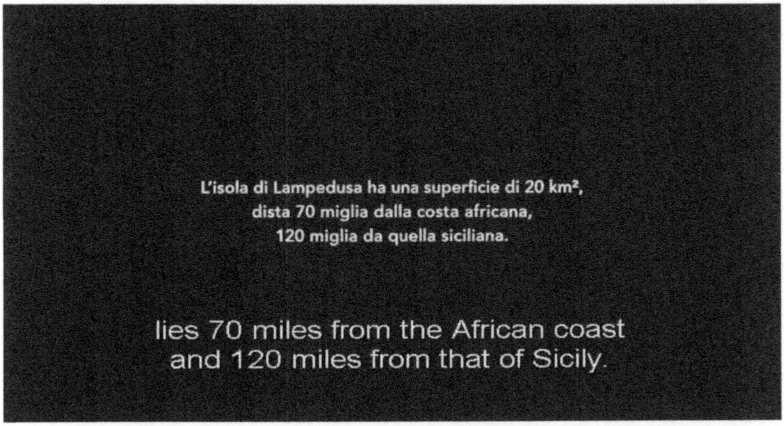

L'isola di Lampedusa ha una superficie di 20 km²,
dista 70 miglia dalla costa africana,
120 miglia da quella siciliana.

lies 70 miles from the African coast
and 120 miles from that of Sicily.

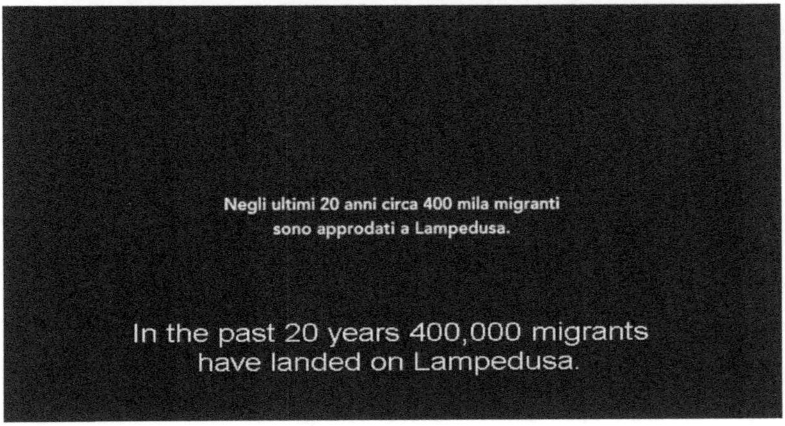

Negli ultimi 20 anni circa 400 mila migranti
sono approdati a Lampedusa.

In the past 20 years 400,000 migrants
have landed on Lampedusa.

Figures 1.6–1.10 The opening titles from *Fire at Sea*

Nel tentativo di attraversare
il Canale di Sicilia per raggiungere l'Europa,
si stima che siano morte 15 mila persone.

In the attempt to cross
the Strait of Sicily to reach Europe

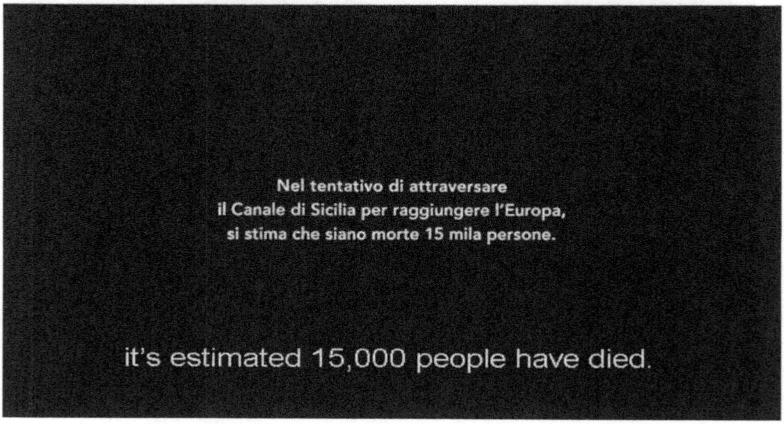

Nel tentativo di attraversare
il Canale di Sicilia per raggiungere l'Europa,
si stima che siano morte 15 mila persone.

it's estimated 15,000 people have died.

Figures 1.6–1.10 Continued

Notes

1. *The Bad Kids*, directed by Keith Fulton and Lou Pepe (Low Key Pictures, 2016), 1:12:34.
2. The term *verité* derives from filmmaker Jean Rouch and Edgar Morin's phrase *cinema verité* ("film truth"), which they coined in 1960 to describe the improvisatory method they used in their film *The Chronicle of a Summer*. In using the phrase they owed a debt to the early Russian filmmaker Dziga Vertov, who called his style of filmmaking *kino pravda* (also "film truth").
3. As these kinds of scenes began to be carried out with more artistry by feature documentary makers in recent decades, other terms like *recreation, restaging*, and *reconstruction* (the term commonly used in the UK), came into being.

4. "Nanook of the North in Five Facts," BBC Radio 3, https://www.bbc.co.uk/programmes/articles/1hXSlq8bHK0VB3cPY7Vrgt2/nanook-of-the-north-in-five-facts#:~:text=Nanook%20is%20an%20extraordinary%20film,North ern%20Quebec%20by%20Robert%20J.

5. Bill Nichols, "Documentary Reenactment and the Fantasmatic Subject," *Critical Inquiry* 35, no. 1 (2008): 72.

6. C. H. Sterling, *Encyclopedia of Journalism* (Los Angeles: Sage Publications, 2009), 1609–16.

7. Walter Goodman, "Connie Chung's 'Saturday' Features James Earl Jones," *New York Times*, September 25, 1989, https://www.nytimes.com/1989/09/25/arts/review-television-connie-chung-s-saturday-features-james-earl-jones.html.

8. NBC News even issued a public statement at the close of the short-lived program that they would thereafter discontinue the use of reenactments. "We just couldn't surmount this issue of viewer confusion," stated NBC News president Michael Gartner. Bill Carter, "NBC-TV to End Dramatizations of News," *New York Times*, November 21, 1989.

9. In fact, one key marker of a scripted docudrama (vs. a documentary) is whether the actors' faces are shown and whether they perform dialogue onscreen.

10. While the fit was natural in some respects, in others it was problematic. As filmmaker Jack Walsh pointed out to me, the fact that a straight black man was chosen to voice the part of James Baldwin, who was gay, arguably had the effect of posthumously recloseting Baldwin.

11. Jeanne Hall, "Realism as a Style in Cinema Verité: A Critical Analysis of *Primary*," in *The Documentary Film Reader: History, Theory, Criticism*, ed. Jonathan Kahana (Oxford: Oxford University Press, 2016), 509.

2
Meaning

In Chapter 1 we discussed the distinct elements of the documentary. In this chapter we will discuss some of the ways that these elements create meaning and how their juxtaposition produces the alchemy that an audience encounters as cinematic experience.

Creating Meaning within the Interview Frame

There is no neutral way of composing and lighting an interview shot. Is the participant bathed in light before a pleasingly de-focused background filled with earthy colors connoting life and nature? Or are there large pools of black in the shot, with deep shadows on the face hiding the person's intentions from the audience? Does the interviewee seem at ease within the frame, or project artificiality, looking straight at us without blinking, almost like a robot, as Elizabeth Holmes does in many interviews in *The Inventor: Out for Blood in Silicon Valley?*[1]

Consider the difference between watching Michael Kimmelman in Amir Bar-Lev's *My Kid Could Paint That* versus John Finlay in Netflix's *Tiger King: Murder, Mayhem, and Madness*, directed by Rebecca Chaiklin and Eric Goode. Kimmelman is seated in his study with his hands clasped calmly before him on a sturdy desk of dark wood (Figure 2.1). Behind him sits a tasteful lamp atop an upright piano, and a wall of custom-built bookcases packed full of large-format art books. He leans forward, clothed in a dignified sport coat and white dress shirt and bathed in soft light. When the lower-third title comes on the screen—"Chief Art Critic, The New York Times"—it is hardly a surprise.

How Documentaries Work. Jacob Bricca, Oxford University Press. © Oxford University Press 2023.
DOI: 10.1093/oso/9780197554104.003.0003

Figure 2.1 Michael Kimmelman in *My Kid Could Paint That*

Figure 2.2 John Finley in *Tiger King: Murder, Mayhem, and Madness*

Finlay also sits in an environment of dark wood, but rather than the sophisticated trappings of a New York City condominium, his domicile looks more like a rustic cabin (Figure 2.2). A tiny kitchen counter and sink stand behind him next to a wood-burning stove. His wooden chair is a partially upholstered recliner, putting him in a La-Z-Boy position that reads doubly odd because of his dress: he is shirtless, tattoos visible all over his chest and arms, small nipple rings protruding from his chest. When he opens his mouth, he reveals only three crooked teeth.

The consequences for the conclusions that we draw about these people could not be more profound, even though they have nothing to do with the content of their testimony. Kimmelman comes across as knowledgeable and literate before he ever opens his mouth. Finlay is depicted as an oddity, something he later expressed displeasure about, noting that the filmmakers had used none of the lengthy follow-up interview he had given after he had received a full set of dentures.[2]

Linda Lee Tracey, a former stripper who appeared as the featured subject of Bonnie Sherr Klein's 1981 film *Not a Love Story: A Film about Pornography*, noted the vastly different background treatments given the antipornography feminists in the film versus sex workers like herself. The feminists were all filmed in middle-class domestic spaces, while the sex workers were filmed in their work environments. "Robin reclines on her sofa with her husband and son . . . charming and welcoming," said Tracey in her book *Growing Up Naked*. "We'll film all the feminists that way," she said, "in their own worlds, surrounded by their trinkets, not swallowed up in ugly places like the porn girls."

Indeed, it is the control over tone that is one distinguishing mark of veteran documentary directors and producers versus ones with less experience. Producer Dan Partland (*The Sixties, The Ballad of Ramblin' Jack*) noted his own early mistakes with shooting on-the-fly interviews on a nonfiction series called *The Residents*, about medical residents in Los Angeles.

This doctor I was shooting was at the depths of her despair as an overworked resident and gave great testimony as I filmed her walking back to her car after she had finished her shift. She was really emotional and said, "I don't know how I can make it through this; how am I going to do this for my *life*?" But as she said this, the background was totally at odds with her emotions. She was walking across a UCLA courtyard on a bright, sunny day with people playing Frisbee in the background, and it just didn't work! You have to have real discipline as a filmmaker not to just ask the question right when you think of it.

Even when setting up interviews on location, experienced filmmakers pay attention to the time of day and the exact lighting available in the room so that they can get a shot that will match the emotions of the topic. While shooting his documentary *The Peacekeepers* about the work of United Nations officials in New York, director Paul Cowan was meticulous about his approach to filming Meg Carey, who directed the UN's peacekeeping operations in the Congo.

I had spent so much time at the UN building in New York that I knew at four o'clock in the afternoon on a certain kind of weather day, if I put Meg in this room the light would be good on her. And I would only film her at that time. . . . I was really careful about where I filmed those people and when I filmed them.

Creating Visual Uniformity with Interviews

Interviews also offer documentarians a valuable opportunity to bring uniformity to their creations. If all interviews carry visual commonalities by shooting them under similar conditions in a studio, this tamps down the sense of chaos and arbitrariness that can quickly overwhelm the visual universe of a documentary. Filmmakers Catherine Ryan, Gary Weimberg, and Judith Leonard used the "black void" style (tasteful soft lighting against a pure black backdrop) in their films *The Story of Mothers and Daughters, The Story of Fathers and Sons,* and *Teens Get Real.* For them, it allowed all of the stories in the films to have similar weight even though the experiences related in the archival footage and verité were extremely varied. For the CNN series *The Sixties,* Producer Dan Partland used the same "black void" look (see Figure 2.3) to maintain consistency across all episodes in the series, in which historians and well-known

Figure 2.3 The "black void" look in *The Sixties*

Figure 2.4 A typical interview in *American Style*

cultural figures pontificate on a variety of subjects, talking about music on one episode and the civil rights movement on the next.

For his later series *American Style*, a show that traced the history of popular fashion in the United States, Partland went a different direction (see Figure 2.4).

The black void had given a unity to *The Sixties,* and we really needed that again since the archival material was coming from so many different sources and was all going to look so different. But we couldn't just do the black void again, because *American Style* wasn't *important* the way some of the topics in *The Sixties* were. It needed to be lighter and funnier, and you had to be able to laugh if someone told a joke. But if it doesn't take itself seriously at all, then the show falls on its face because you have to be able to make meaty, important conclusions about culture based on this.

So, we built a set and erected it in both New York and LA, where we were conducting the interviews. It was just a suggestion of a room: just a wall, with some trim moldings and wainscotting, but it also had an Eames lounger next to a modern tulip table in the background. The twist was we wanted to make sure the background didn't call *too* much attention to itself, so we kept everything on the set white and gray. It was really effective, because it made the subjects look really vibrant, and it made the pictures of the fashion really stand out. It had an iconic style while still being variable.

Another way to get a uniform background is to simply shoot the interview against a green screen and then insert the background later. This has been used many times by producer Amy Ziering for her recent films *The Bleeding Edge* and *On the Record.*

On *The Bleeding Edge,* which is about dangerous medical devices, we wanted our expert interviews to all have specialized backgrounds evocative of a powerful medical industry, and achieving this look would be hard to get otherwise. Also, green screen can often be more economically efficient because the subjects can all travel to you at a single location.

Green screen shooting is common these days and is getting harder and harder to distinguish from interviews shot on location. The ethics of placing interviewees in a space that they never actually inhabited are, of course, complex. In the preceding two cases the participants are placed within abstract backgrounds that do not connote a specific geographical location, but there are cases from other documentaries in which this blending has occurred.

Creating Meaning with Objects in the Frame

What can be said by the objects that accompany the participant in the interview frame? A first viewing of *Tiger King* likely has the audience transfixed by the unapologetic display of outrageous behavior by its protagonists, but a closer look also reveals an extraordinary number of animal figurines placed in the interview shots—a rooster here, a monkey there, a glass coffee table supported by an enormous glazed ceramic lion—each one upping the ante on the overall impression of humans obsessed with other species (see Figure 2.5). Music documentaries often place the artists in the middle of a highly staged composition with their arm draped over their instrument. (Is this how they go about their day, with their guitar slung over their shoulder?)

By the same token, the careful arrangement of objects in noninterview shots is also a way of making meaning. "Having two large empty beds is twice as depressing as having one large empty bed," complains a lonely Ross McElwee from a shabby motel room in

Figure 2.5 A lion and a monkey populate the interview frame in *Tiger King*

his comedic and painfully personal *Sherman's March*.[3] He is framed as a small figure cowering in the corner of one of two queen beds; the camera is placed all the way on the other side of the second bed, which looks massive and forlorn, and the effect is instant comedy. The sense of scale is also repeatedly felt in Godfrey Reggio's poetic masterpieces *Koyaanisqatsi* and *Powaqqatsi*, in shots of tiny human figures dwarfed by the machines of the modern world, which helps build his portrait of humanity on the brink of environmental and spiritual collapse from a rapacious world capitalist system run amok. In one scene from *Powaqqatsi* a small boy walks on the side of a dirt road toward the camera. As he is overtaken by a massive truck (anonymous, with only part of its huge frame visible) a huge cloud of dust envelops him. The shot has eerie similarities to a shot in *Koyaanisqatsi* where the operator of a huge construction vehicle is enveloped by a massive cloud of dark dust that blocks out the sun and turns the frame a ghostly dark gray. This impulse to build meaning with the clever arrangement of objects within the frame is part of a long documentary tradition going back to films such as *The Plow That Broke the Plains* (1936), which turned tractors and threshing machines into symbols of exploitative excess as they mercilessly worked the soil of the Great Plains states until it could give no more, resulting in the Dust Bowl calamity of the 1930s.

Creating Meaning with Words

For all the meaning imparted through purely visual means, words are often the dominant element of meaning creation in documentaries. Consider the following experience of watching an iconic documentary from the 1980s with the sound turned off: a young boy in a 1950s outfit is seen smiling goofily at the camera in vivid color. Cut to a black-and-white still image of a male musician on his knees playing the electric guitar. Cut to a headshot of 1980s radio personality Casey Kasem, a shot of a classical music conductor with baton in hand, and headshots of the actor Don Knotts and game show host Bob Eubanks. Images of the front page of the *Flint Voice* and archival footage of someone standing in front of the offices of the *Michigan Voice* float by. Cut to the Golden Gate Bridge.

What the hell is going on? Watching this ninety-second section of Michael Moore's classic 1989 documentary *Roger and Me* without the help of the soundtrack proves a simple lesson: many documentaries derive a huge quotient of their meaning from the spoken word.[4] The images alone seem arbitrary and comically unrelated on their own, but with the soundtrack engaged they instantly make sense. "The assembly line wasn't for me," Moore narrates over the picture of the young boy that we now clearly understand to be Moore himself. "My heroes were the people who had escaped the life in the factory and got out of Flint," he says while a series of archival shots of the once-famous glide across the screen. "[People] like the guys in Grand Funk Railroad; Casey Kasem; the women who married [classical music conductor] Zubin Mehta; Don Knotts; and perhaps Flint's most famous native son Bob Eubanks, the host of TV's hit show *The Newlywed Game*." Pausing for comedic effect, he continues: "I figured if Bob Eubanks could make it out of here, so could I." Over the newspaper shots he says, "After ten years of editing my own paper in Flint, a California millionaire asked me to be the editor of his muckraking magazine in San Francisco." The Golden Gate Bridge sparkles in the sun.

In this documentary strategy, the primary role is given to the narrator in what is essentially an illustrated lecture. Listening to the narration on its own is less satisfying than watching the finished film, but it is not fundamentally confusing or frustrating. Words lead the creation of meaning; pictures *confirm and elaborate on* that meaning. This regimen is as old as documentary filmmaking itself, as David MacDougall points out when referring to 1930s classics like *Song of Ceylon* and *The City*: "Each of the discrete images in such documentaries was the bearer of a pre-determined meaning."[5] Try making sense of *My Octopus Teacher* without the voice track and prepare yourself for an utterly unsatisfying experience.

This is not to say that the creation of such meaning is an unsophisticated endeavor. An analysis of a nineteen-second scene from Raoul Peck's *I Am Not Your Negro* shows the delicate dance between picture

Figure 2.6 Dorothy Counts in *I Am Not Your Negro*

and narration as they intermingle.[6] The audience sees a still image of an African American teenage girl, which widens out to reveal a crowd of young men gathered around her (see Figure 2.6). Narrator Samuel L. Jackson, voicing James Baldwin, speaks: "That's when I saw the photograph on every newspaper kiosk on that wide, tree-shaped boulevard in Paris: photographs of fifteen-year-old Dorothy Counts being reviled and spat upon by the mob as she was making her way to school in Charlotte, North Carolina." By this time the film has cut to a second photo. There is no spitting shown—this is left to the imagination—but the word "reviled" lands hard as it nudges the audience to notice the self-satisfied grins and hints of malice on the faces in the crowd. "There was unutterable pride, tension, and anguish as she approached the halls of learning," Jackson continues, as all three emotions are indeed evident on her face. The film then cuts to the most provocative and upsetting photo so far: Counts is surrounded in a medium shot by young men who are ridiculing her from behind as Jackson concludes, "with history jeering at her back."

Let's look a little deeper into how meaning is created in this scene. First, Peck's direction of Samuel L. Jackson's narration removes much of the swagger that accompanied his roles in films like *Pulp Fiction* and *Snakes on a Plane* in favor of a tone of weary but determined resolve. This dissociates the narration from distracting references to

Hollywood blockbusters and makes it possible to put James Baldwin directly into the scene even though he never appears onscreen. As the pictures begin to grace the screen, the audience now sees what he saw ("That's when I saw the photograph") via a moving vignette effect on the photos. This turns a simple photo into a subjective experience of looking through Baldwin's eyes as he scans the photos. The words also carry some poetic license that expands their meaning beyond the literal: "halls of learning" evokes a more general and sweeping idea than just a literal entrance to a facility, and "history jeering at her back" puts the events into world-historical context that evokes an epic battle for justice rather than just a single shot of some boys shouting at a girl. Seen on their own, the pictures do not tell a story—the emotions that show on her face could be read in a number of ways. It is the specification of "pride, tension, and anguish" from the narration that draws those emotions out of the image, like a sorcerer conjuring spirits from an inanimate object. The pictures supply the "evidence," but the narration draws out of them what the filmmaker intends from the scene, leaving alternate meanings unexplored. As Bill Nichols notes of this "expository" mode of documentary filmmaking, "Each shot serves to represent typical qualities needed to support the film's point of view,"[7] which is largely determined by the voice.

A piece of narration in the Academy Award nominee *The Edge of Democracy* provides similar shading to ambiguous images. Director Petra Costa narrates crucial decades in the political life of her native Brazil, where politicians from the Far Right cynically pursued the impeachment of the president, Dilma Rousseff, by making highly misleading claims about her ties to a corruption scandal. On the screen is a seemingly innocuous piece of pageantry from years past as Rousseff walks in a victory parade beside her newly elected vice president, Michel Temer.[8] But the images take on entirely new meaning with Costa's narration. "Today, looking back," she says with audible lament, "I realize the excitement of having elected our first female president blinded me to . . . the precipice that exists between Rousseff and her tense vice president." Up to this moment the audience has scarcely noticed him, looking instead at the joy being expressed by Rousseff as she savors the historic moment. Looking

Figure 2.7 Narration draws attention to the physical distance between Dilma Rousseff and Michel Temer in The Edge of Democracy

more carefully, one can notice a physical distance between her and Temer as he walks with a forced smile beside her (see Figure 2.7). "[He] has his gestures controlled," Costa continues, "as if he's moving inside a box. He interlocks his fingers and pulls his hands, as if he wanted to separate them." The reevaluation is staggering because the narration has completely changed the meaning of the clip, and the audience will soon learn that Temer was instrumental in later ousting Rousseff from power.

In documentaries featuring reenactments, words again play a crucial role in defining their meaning. As we discussed in Chapter 1, reenactments are usually shot with deliberately partial and disadvantaged viewpoints, which has the effect of reserving a large amount of the meaning creation for the spoken word. The blend of elements fuses in the audience's imagination to build an experience that is simultaneously real and unreal, with the interview audio acting as the real element that narrates the visuals, which are marked as an interpretation. An odd paradox is that while the authority/authenticity of the voice is bolstered in this arrangement, the entire experience falls apart if the audience's attention is drawn too strongly to the circumstances under which the voice recording was made. Audio recorded with echoey sound or too much background noise is a deal-breaker precisely because it places the viewer firmly in the space and time when it was recorded, disallowing the mental blending; it's *too* authentic to function as "real."

Interview-as-Narration

As we have seen, a sequence anchored by narration will inevitably relegate images to a secondary role in the creation of meaning. Yet the voice dominates in a huge variety of documentaries, not just ones featuring a traditional narrator. Much more often these days, the *interview subjects* become the de facto narrators, speaking in their own voices but still fulfilling the same basic function of a narrator. The audience may see the interviewees onscreen (as in more traditional documentaries) or their voices may be utilized without any visual reference to the interview (as in more contemporary films like *Amy* or *Senna* from filmmaker Asif Kapadia), but either way the words are put in the driver's seat. Let's look at some of the meaning creation in films that feature interview-as-narration and note just how precise the sound/image pairings are.

Early in *The Kingmaker*, Lauren Greenfield's disturbing account of Imelda Marcos's return to influence in the Philippines, Marcos describes being unhappy in her early role as First Lady when her husband Ferdinand Marcos ruled the country under martial law from 1972 to 1981. The sequence starts with a close-up interview shot and then cuts to three short archival image cutaways that give confirmatory evidence for her words (see Table 2.1).

The entire sequence takes just twenty-one seconds, and the money shot of Marcos looking miserable while shaking hands is on the screen for just four seconds, but note how the apex of her unhappiness—the pause after "I had to do this, I had to do that"—coincides perfectly with the shot of her looking tense and worried (see Figure 2.8).[9]

The shot is a tiny fragment of recorded history, surely with its own idiosyncratic reason for why she was looking unhappy at this particular moment. (Physical illness? Too hot? Crowd noise too loud?) Used in this context, however, it creates a much more sweeping impression

Table 2.1 Words and Images in *The Kingmaker*

Interview-as-narration (creates the meaning)	Image (confirms the meaning)
In the beginning I was having a hard time, because here in this house there were always plenty of people, and I was not used to that.	Close-up interview shot
(Pause)	Archival black-and-white still of Imelda cutting a ribbon at a ceremony
Everything became so public,	[Shot continues]
I had to cut ribbons, I had to . . .	Second black-and-white archival image of Marcos cutting a ribbon at a ceremony, a forced smile on her face
do this, I had to do that. (Pause)	Marcos shaking hands with someone, looking miserable
It came to a point that . . .	[Shot continues, slow zoom on her unhappy face]
I could not take politics.	Close-up interview shot

Figure 2.8 Imelda Marcos in *The Kingmaker*

of her feelings about being the First Lady. With pictures as proof, the audience is meant to conclude that her difficulties were real, and at this moment in the film they are encouraged to feel sympathy for her.[10]

A close variant of this approach uses visual evidence directly *after* the statement rather than simultaneous to it—the audience hears an assertion, and then visual evidence follows to back it up. One of the many colorful characters in *Tiger King: Murder, Mayhem, and Madness* is Bhagavan "Doc" Antle, owner of a "big cat" zoo in Myrtle Beach, Florida, who describes himself thusly in Episode 1: "I am popular. I am so well known as . . . being this guy that is in love with big cats and has them love him back."[11] As if to confirm the truth of this statement, the subsequent shot is of Antle feeding a huge white tiger a massive bottle of milk. The tiger gently nuzzles its head on Antle's shoulder.

A significant portion of *Tiger King*'s structure is built around this pattern, with each statement paired with a confirmatory scene, operating as dyads as the story progresses. Contrasts are set up between opposing points of view by letting one side have its say and then confirming its ostensible validity, only to have an opposing statement follow it with *its* own piece of "evidence." Note that the evidence in the confirming scene functions that way because the audience is primed to interpret it this way *just because of its placement.* (Taking a closer look at the confirmatory clip of Antle feeding the tiger shows that it may not confirm what it seems to: watching the clip carefully, one sees that the tiger is clearly enjoying the meal but is somewhat indifferent to the man supplying the sustenance. Such is the power of words, especially when the pace of the show is as assertive as *Tiger King*, which makes it nearly impossible for the audience to absorb the subtleties of each moment.)

Priming the audience with a piece of interview-as-narration to elicit a particular interpretation is not a trick reserved for sensationalistic docuseries like *Tiger King*. It is also used in Steve James's *The Interrupters* (Figure 2.9). As James says:

> Sometimes the strategic placement of a line of voice-over can make a huge difference. For instance, in *The Interrupters* there's a really entertaining scene where Cobe approaches this guy Flamo, who is black, for

Figure 2.9 Flamo in *The Interrupters*

the first time. Flamo is frustrated and a little drunk and all of a sudden throws his cell phone into the snow. I remember thinking when I shot it that it was pretty funny. But in test screenings it got really different reactions from black audiences and white audiences. Black audiences thought it was hilarious, but white audiences never laughed because they didn't feel like they had the permission to do so.

So I went back and got Cobe to give me a line of voice-over that plays near the beginning of the scene that establishes two things: that Flamo's been in and out of prison most of his life, and that he's funny. Cobe says, "Flamo can be a funny guy, but you don't want to mess with him, you know?" So that was our way of giving audiences permission to laugh and enjoy the scene for its entertainment value, but also hopefully not dismiss him as just some guy who is playacting for the camera and is not for real. Basically we were trying to frame the scene and guide them to how they might want to react to it.[12]

Creating Meaning with Verité

The preceding examples have focused on pictures matched with narration or interview-as-narration. But the role given to images as bearers of confirmatory meanings also applies to pure cinema verité scenes. Verité scenes have an unmistakable aura of authenticity to them, seeming to replicate the chaos, unpredictability, and energy of real-life conversations, as we noted in Chapter 1. Yet the picture/sound combinations that produce this feeling are anything but random. A scene that I edited from the 2010 film *Small Farm Rising* serves as an example.[13]

Ian Ater and Lucas Christenson are the proprietors of Fledging Crow Farm, a small produce operation in upstate New York. Standing in sweaty T-shirts that betray a hard day's work, they are hashing out what to do about a customer who is squeezing them on prices. "What's our lowball?" says Ian to Lucas with a calculator in his hand.

"If we do a buck thirty-five that gives us four hundred a bed," muses Lucas, a hint of annoyance in his voice at having to play this game when their margins are already so low. "I think we can go as low as a buck thirty-five."

Cut to a cramped and messy office space as Ian picks up the phone—it's their customer.[14] As Ian proceeds with the delicate negotiation, the cutaway shots to Lucas are a crucial element in bringing added tension and emotional depth to the scene as well as providing a way to hide the dialogue edits.

"How are you, Water Dog?" says Ian cheerfully into the phone (Figure 2.10). The use of the nickname and casual tone of voice suggest a benign interaction, but this is just the text; the subtext is provided by the cutaway to Lucas settling into his chair, taking off his sunglasses and looking up at Ian with great seriousness, as if to say, *Okay, let's settle in because this might get ugly* (Figure 2.11).

After a quick back-and-forth about the availability of broccoli rabe, there is a cut to Ian. "Do you need any romaine this week?" he asks. On its own it's an innocent question, but the cutaway to Lucas turns it into a moment of great anticipation as his eyes shift to and fro, dreading the coming clash. "We're asking a buck thirty-five," says Ian expectantly as Lucas's expression seems to say, *Aha, the moment of truth* (Figure 2.12).

There is a pause on the other end. Cut back to Ian who awkwardly fills the silence: "They're gigantic, though!" The final cutaway of

Figure 2.10 Ian answers the phone in *Small Farm Rising*

Figure 2.11 Lucas reacts with anticipation in *Small Farm Rising*

Lucas adds a note of defiance as he looks wistfully offscreen and nods to himself, as if to say, *Take it or leave it, but our romaine is as good as it gets* (Figure 2.13).

Cut back to Ian, whose face looks ashen as he listens to silence on the other end of the line (Figure 2.14). Cut to black.

What we have seen here is that picture/sound interactions are powerfully persuasive, generating specific neurocognitive activity in the

Figure 2.12 The moment of truth in *Small Farm Rising*

Figure 2.13 Lucas, proud of the Fledging Crow product in *Small Farm Rising*

audience because of the precise timing of their juxtaposition. The looks on Lucas's face are timed to fill in the gaps in meaning and push the scene in a particular direction. In actuality, some of the cutaways in this scene were stolen from completely unrelated moments in the conversation. The final cutaway of Lucas looking proud of his high-quality lettuce, for instance, comes from a moment when Lucas was talking with Ian about their long friendship. The juxtaposition offered by the film

Figure 2.14 A final look of apprehension from Ian in *Small Farm Rising*

is not technically false (since it is helping express very real anxieties as experienced by the two friends) but is not fully true either. The power of the editing is such that Ian and Lucas were themselves utterly convinced of the authenticity of the scene when they saw the final product, and commented upon how perfectly it depicted the challenges, frustrations, and intense emotions of running their small business.

This paradox is one that is at the heart of documentary's power— and its contradictions. Many documentarians fall back on the old axiom that "art is a lie that tells the truth," a quotation which has been attributed in various forms to Pablo Picasso, Neil Gaiman, and Albert Camus, among others, in defending their manipulations. They might today refer to Colson Whitehead, who gave a full-throated commitment to "the truth of things, not the facts"[15] when discussing his novel of historical fiction *The Underground Railroad*, about the network of people who offered shelter and aid to escaped enslaved people from the South. Barry Jenkins, who directed the filmed adaptation, took the same liberties. In discussing his approach, Jenkins said the following:

> There was an article that came out about two months ago about this textbook that was still being used in [the South] that was telling high

school students that American slavery was a system of conscripted labor. . . . It was being framed in this way. And I realized, "Oh, if I had only read the *fiction* of Toni Morrison as a high school student, I would have gotten closer to the truth . . . than reading this fact-based textbook."[16]

It is useful for viewers to know that many documentarians think of their work in terms similar to those of historical fiction, as opposed to that of journalism. Any time you encounter a particularly poignant moment in a verité scene, it is worth thinking about how that impression was generated and to remember that the elements may have been taken from unrelated sources. As long as it is expressing the *emotional* truth of the participants in her collaboration with them, it is seen as fair game. As we will discuss in the section on *The Cave* and *For Sama* in Chapter 9, it is crucial to consider the institutional context of the film. *Frontline* and Channel 4, for instance, have different standards with respect to the liberties taken in editing than many documentaries made by independent filmmakers or produced by Netflix.

Open versus Closed Meanings

A crucial thing to note about the voice-dominated approach to documentary storytelling is that it tends to be correlated with "closed" meanings. The highly synchronized nature of the picture/voice interaction means that the audience is led quickly from one nugget of meaning to the next, with little time to truly evaluate them. As MacDougall notes, "We are invited to participate in creating the meaning of each shot by recognizing its narrative or expository center. The length of each shot is gauged so that we must carry this out fairly quickly, leaving little time for other considerations."[17] Indeed, a crucial talent of a skilled editor is to determine the smallest amount of time that an image must remain on the screen for the audience member to decipher the meaning that the shot is meant to deliver, then move on to the next one.

The practice is similar to editing conventions in fiction films. In his 1984 book on narrative film editing, Edward Dmytryk delivered this piece of advice to young editors:

> The first shot has played itself out on the screen. . . . To linger on it after our actor has left the scene is to leave our viewer with "cold coffee." . . . If the viewer is not confused or disappointed, he will simply be bored. It has been many years since a mere picture projected on the screen was considered amazing or amusing. Every part of a film must deliver its message, but the only message delivered by redundant frames of film is that the cutter was inept or too lazy to cut them off.[18]

This makes explicit what is implicit in the dominant cutting style of our age: that a single meaning accompanies each shot and that our job as viewers is to identify it, consume it, and move on. This environment of meaning creation is much like the experience of video games built around treasure collection such as Nintendo's Super Mario Bros. series, in which the player (as Mario) travels in forward motion through a predetermined maze, collecting coins, Super Mushrooms, and Fire Flowers along the way.[19] Each goodie delivers a little burst of pleasure for Mario in the form of a pleasing ping of sound. The pleasure from the treasure is quickly crushed and consumed, however, and Mario must instantly move on to the next microgoal. The point of a game like this is not to admire the scenery along the way (though the Day-Glo colors and psychedelic touches certainly make it appealing), but rather to push forward toward the ultimate goal.

This way of making meaning turns documentary sequences into closed systems, with predetermined sets of reactions that the film anticipates from its audience. The relentless push forward precludes "meaning in excess of what the film expresses and requires" and constitutes "a closing off . . . of areas in which the viewer is invited to supply meaning," states MacDougall. Filmmaker Jill Godmilow describes the conundrum in these terms: a sequence with closed meanings "can't dream. It can't provoke imagination."

David MacDougall associates this tendency with the way documentary developed as an art form though history.

The great enemy of documentary is the "dead spot" in which nothing seems to be happening. Film producers are terrified of such moments, for they are terrified of audience impatience. I suspect that the taboo status of this topic goes back to an inherent contradiction in documentary principles.

Documentary, whatever its ideology, still took its shape from fiction or journalism. It had to defend its interest in the ordinary by making sure that the ordinary played well. Who cared to admit that documentary actually concealed the lacunae characteristic of ordinary life and chose only the best bits, just like fiction filmmakers?[20]

By striving to keep up with the visceral emotional density of more traditional forms of narrative filmmaking, MacDougall concludes, documentary took on many of its conventions.

Not all documentary filmmakers work in this way. Filmmaker J. P. Sniadecki, known for films with long takes and lots of interpretive space, explains his feelings about conventional documentary filmmaking thusly:

What I find really frustrating about a lot of documentaries that are quite successful commercially is that I am never really given a moment to *see* an image. I'm only seeing the edits and I'm only seeing the argumentation. One of the great things about the long take is that it's not trying to close meaning; it's not trying to make an argument that's unidirectional. It's actually inviting a more active, more dialogical relationship to the material onscreen that opens up different kinds of interpretive relationships.

For a prime example of this wholly different relationship between audience and filmmaker, consider the mesmerizing 2016 documentary *Another Year*, directed by Shengze Zhu and featuring a year in the life of a Chinese family. Composed of just thirteen shots over its 181-minute running time, each shot shows the family eating a meal around their small dining room table; the camera never moves. This likely sounds like the recipe for a dull film, but it is anything but.

The first scene opens with a child of about six watching cartoons in a small room that appears to be lit by a single fluorescent light. As she sits in her chair, eyes glued to the screen, one difference between this documentary and most others is quickly made clear: instead of the image providing a single point of focus, it has two. The child and the television sit on opposite edges of the frame and, to absorb the full scope of the shot, one must look back and forth repeatedly. There is more information being offered than it is possible to absorb at any one moment; viewers are thus left to decide how to apportion their attention. They might also find themselves looking around the other parts of the frame to find a small table on the right, a modest second table in the back, and a small mountain of other objects piled against the back wall (see Figure 2.15). All these things hold meaning for the story to come.

At forty-one seconds into the shot, a girl of about thirteen enters the frame, sits down on a chair near the television, and takes in its incessant chatter. Twenty seconds later, an elderly woman enters slowly and sits near the back, a tired look on her face. By now three people are in the frame, and the audience begins to make inferences about their relationship (granddaughter, granddaughter, grandmother?) and also may note that all three are wearing heavy coats. The outside world, though never shown, is referenced repeatedly throughout the film in subtle ways like this one.

Figure 2.15 A scene from *Another Year*

Note how this form of information delivery differs from conventional films. In a conventional film, the audience is led down a single path and presented with a story that unfolds as a series of consecutive revelations, each of which deepens the story. The moments do refer back to information revealed earlier and the growing story can build in depth and complexity, but the moments themselves tend to be singular bursts of precise meaning. In *Another Year*, many of the meanings are sitting side by side at any given moment, waiting for the audience to discover them at their own pace. Other meanings develop chronologically—the characters enter one by one, for instance—but because the film displays all the characters in the same frame at once rather than cutting between them, there is vastly more potential meaning in the frame at any given moment (see Figure 2.16).

This alternate role for the audience is consistent with some fiction films made for the international art house market. Note the similar observations about meaning made by *L.A. Times* film critic Justin Chang in a discussion of the 2021 Chaitanya Tamhane film *The Disciple*.

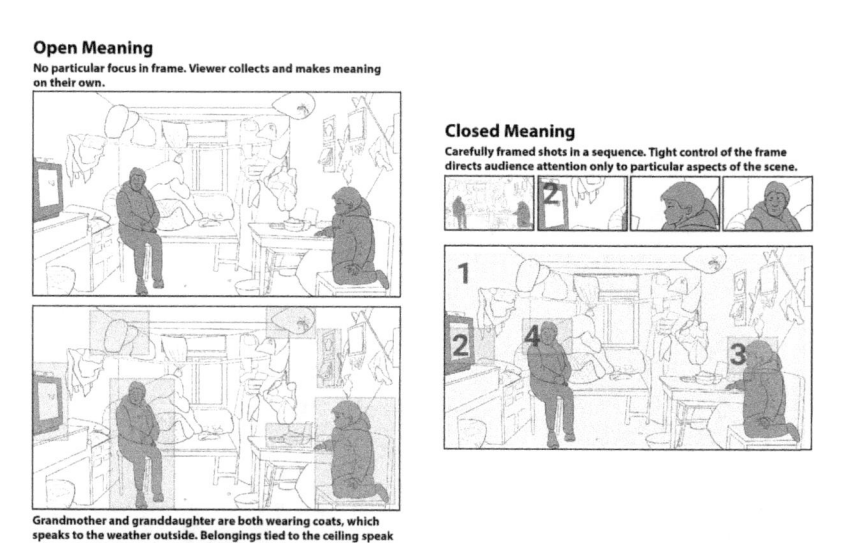

Open Meaning
No particular focus in frame. Viewer collects and makes meaning on their own.

Closed Meaning
Carefully framed shots in a sequence. Tight control of the frame directs audience attention only to particular aspects of the scene.

Grandmother and granddaughter are both wearing coats, which speaks to the weather outside. Belongings tied to the ceiling speak to the temporary nature of the dwelling. Calendar hints at the months in the year-long journey of the family.

Figure 2.16 Open meanings vs. closed meanings in *Another Year*
Illustration by Kaylah Rasmussen.

[A lot of the meaning in the film comes from master shots.] And I think that that is where a lot of the wisdom and the nuance of this movie comes from, because there's something about a long take where you're seeing . . . bodies in a room. It allows for all these different tones and inflections to come through. The movie is not just splicing reality into little bits and shoving them at you, like one idea for per frame. No, it's like there's five or maybe ten ideas per frame.[21]

Another Year is filled with indelible moments that function simultaneously as character development, social realist observations, and hints at the larger world of the family's life beyond the edges of the frame (see Figure 2.14). A smile from the grandmother shows a single crooked tooth, deepening the audience's understanding of the family's class status; the sound of a modern train chugging by is heard, giving a hint as to the urban nature of the locale; bags of belongings hang from the ceiling, giving another indication of this dwelling's impermanent nature; a calendar sits on the wall, subtly drawing attention to the possible meaning of the title.

Once the mother is introduced and the father finally arrives, the mother delivers a bluntly vicious denunciation of the grandmother (her mother-in-law), demanding that Father "send her back to the village," and insisting that "she's fucking annoying" because she contributes so little to the running of the household. When mom leaves the frame to get more food from the offscreen kitchen, grandmother is silent for a while but then gently pleads her case to her son by complaining that she had to go up and down the stairs three times that day and that "the blankets need to be aired out" (perhaps laying a bit of subtle blame for the oversight at the feet of her daughter-in-law.)

As the film proceeds, each of the subsequent single-shot scenes reveals something new about the location as the drama between the characters also unfolds. Some things change—the mother and grandmother show a tender familiarity at times that seems like it might transcend the bitterness between them—and others remain firmly the same: the middle daughter watches television in nearly every shot and the dad drinks a single bottle of the same brand of beer without fail at every meal. Clues to their hopes and dreams are scattered throughout the experience, as the audience slowly learns that they travel back and forth between their original home in the countryside and the crowded urban apartment that serves as a second home while mother and father work in the factories. The title that comes up at the end—*Another Year*—gently hints at the relative lack of social mobility of the family, even as minor victories are experienced along the way.

Another example of open meanings can be found in scenes from the 2019 Academy Award nominee *Hale County This Morning, This Evening*, a poetic meditation on black identity in Hale County, Alabama. The approach announces itself in one of the first title cards:

What is the orbit of our dreaming?

The question is not of the highly specific variety that we will discuss in Chapter 3. (*Which chef on Hell's Kitchen will be safe from elimination?*) It is broader and more poetic. Like *Another Year*, it invites active viewing to peer into the images and find meaning. While most scenes in *Hale County* are on the screen for relatively short amounts of time and have well-defined points of focus within the frame, the shots themselves are often ambiguous in their meaning and do not follow each other in a cause-and-effect fashion, instead showing small vignettes of relatively ordinary events (basketball practice, a birthday party, a haircut) with a large number of characters. The vignettes are rich with the small joys of life in a tight-knit community. To wit:

- A sixty-three-second driving shot as the camera makes its way slowly down the center of a street lined with folks waiting for a parade. There is no single specific meaning to be plucked. The audience is simply meant to observe.
- A 110-second moving-camera shot of endless fields of cotton as the audience hears sounds from a Selma University basketball game. The meaning is multidimensional, given the lead-in from the monologues by two young men about their life aspirations and the oblique reference to the days of slavery with the shot of cotton.

Figure 2.17 A scene from *Hale County This Morning, This Evening*

- A short scene at a birthday party that includes a seven-second shot of the main subject sitting on a sofa, his head perfectly obscured by a balloon hanging from the ceiling (Figure 2.17).[22] In a film focused on closed meanings, this shot would be removed because it frustrates a desire for quick comprehension and simple meaning.

Here meaning is built through accretion rather than as a single unfolding narrative. Thus, the film tends toward the pleasures of metaphor and poetry rather than of "finding out," and each scene has multiple meanings rather than a single one.

Notes

1. The eerie footage of Holmes staring unblinkingly into the camera is actually raw footage shot by Errol Morris for a promotional campaign for Theranos, the disgraced company founded by Holmes.
2. Thatiana Diaz, "Tiger King's John Finlay Shows Off His New Smile—& Tells Us What the Show Got Wrong," *Refinery 29*, April 13, 2020, https://www.refiner y29.com/en-us/2020/04/9684384/john-finlay-tiger-king-new-teeth-interview.

3. *Sherman's March: A Meditation on the Possibility of Romantic Love in the South during an Era of Nuclear Weapons Proliferation*, directed by Ross McElwee (First Run Features, 1985), 00:32:57.

4. *Roger & Me*, directed by Michael Moore (Warner Brothers, 1989), 00:04:13.

5. David MacDougall, *Transcultural Cinema* (Princeton, NJ: Princeton University Press, 1998), 128.

6. *I Am Not Your Negro*, directed by Raoul Peck (Magnolia Pictures, 2016), 00:06:58.

7. Bill Nichols, *Speaking Truths with Film: Evidence, Ethics, Politics in Documentary* (Oakland: University of California Press, 2016), 76.

8. *The Edge of Democracy*, directed by Petra Costa (Busca Vida Films, 2019), 00:22.44.

9. *The Kingmaker*, directed by Lauren Greenfield (Showtime Documentary Films, 2019), 00:09:44.

10. The film later exposes massive corruption and self-dealing and portrays Marcos in a less sympathetic light.

11. *Tiger King: Murder, Mayhem, and Madness*, Episode 1, directed by Eric Goode and Rebecca Chaiklin (2020), 00:21:30.

12. *The Interrupters*, directed by Steve James (Kartemquin Films, 2011), 1:14:28.

13. The description that follows is a condensation of the scene for brevity's sake. *Small Farm Rising*, directed by Ben Stechschulte (Mountain Lake PBS, 2012), 00:16:39.

14. In actual fact, it was not the same customer as the one they were discussing when they were prepping for the call. It was a different customer, but the haggling over prices was a common occurrence, and this one was used because the footage was better than the interaction with the actual customer.

15. Andrew Purcell, "Colson Whitehead: 'The Truth of Things, Not the Facts,'" *Sydney Morning Herald*, May 11, 2017, https://www.smh.com.au/entertainm ent/books/colson-whitehead-the-truth-of-things-not-the-facts-20170511- gw2bud.html.

16. Podcast interview with Barry Jenkins, "WTF with Marc Maron," Episode 1255, August 23, 2021.

17. MacDougall, *Transcultural Cinema*, 213.

18. Edward Dmytryk, *On Film Editing* (Boston: Focal Press, 1984), 36–37.

19. To be even more specific, it most closely resembles older versions of the game when Mario had a more direct forward path through the worlds. In more recent versions of the game the player has more options for exploring alternate paths.

20. MacDougall, *Transcultural Cinema*, 211.

21. Slate Culture Gabfest podcast, May 12, 2021.

22. *Hale County This Morning, This Evening*, directed by RaMell Ross (Louverture Films, 2018), 00:04:33.

3
Narrative

The urge to narrate is as old as humanity itself; there are no known human cultures that do not engage in storytelling. Every time we explain something to a friend or loved one, we give an interpretive gloss on our experience. Narrative "ceaselessly substitutes meaning for the straightforward copy of the events recounted," noted Hayden White in 1980 in his seminal essay "The Value of Narrativity in the Representation of Reality."[1] We are constantly telling our own stories, telling stories about others, and consuming stories via the various media we ingest. Newspaper articles aren't called "stories" by accident, after all.

In the essay, White tries to get at what distinguishes narrative from other forms of information delivery by comparing the Annals of Saint Gall from the eighth century against later works of history. The annals simply recount a chronological list of events in Gaul (present-day France), as seen in this excerpt covering the years AD 709–722.

709. Hard winter. Duke Gottfried died.
710. Hard year and deficient in crops.
711.
712. Flood everywhere.
713.
714. Pippin, mayor of the palace, died.
715.
716.
717.
718. Charles devastated the Saxon with great destruction.
719.

How Documentaries Work. Jacob Bricca, Oxford University Press. © Oxford University Press 2023.
DOI: 10.1093/oso/9780197554104.003.0004

720. Charles fought against the Saxons.
721. Theudo drove the Saracens out of Aquitaine.
722. Great crops.

Nothing links the events, and there is no interpretive spin. As White says, there is "no central subject, no well-marked beginning, middle, and end . . . and no identifiable narrative voice." Reading the annals, one may try to construct a cause-and-effect relationship between the events, but the document itself steadfastly refuses to do so. By contrast, one finds a stronger voice of authorship in later works of historical writing via a desire to build plot and story, a willingness to tell events out of a strict forward-moving chronological sequence, as well as the insertion of a moral dimension that places implicit or explicit value judgments on the actions of the subjects.

Narrativizing events, then, is the process of building causality and attaching meaning to heretofore inert facts. As White says in the conclusion of his essay:

> [Narrativity] arises out of a desire to have real events display the coherence, integrity, fullness, and closure of an image of life that is and can only be imaginary. . . . Does the world really present itself to perception in the form of well-made stories, with central subjects, proper beginnings, middles, and ends, and a coherence that permits us to see "the end" in every beginning? Or does it present itself more in the forms that the annals . . . suggest, either as mere sequence without beginning or end or as sequences of beginnings that only terminate and never conclude?

By focusing meaning—highlighting certain material, excluding other material, and rearranging it in order to produce a story—documentary launches into the realm of the semifictional because the logic of stories is not necessarily the logic of real life. The power of the narrative ideal—the hero (or antihero) confronting an obstacle and rising to defeat (or succumbing to) it—is a structure so familiar that many audience members hardly notice its existence in the documentaries they watch. But it takes work to produce and arrange stories with these attributes, and that ideal is only one of many ways to get at the truth. Troubling is the degree to which audiences judge a documentary's credibility largely based on the degree to which it conforms to narrative logic, rather than on its other merits. As Manfred W. Becker says:

> People receive or reject narratives based on a test: Do they make sense as story constructions? Do the characters behave coherently, and is the narrative trustworthy? The degree to which we believe [a character] is determined by how faithfully it seems to represent what a character "would" do.[2]

In the rest of this chapter, we will break down the editorial work necessary to create such story constructions, as well as exploring documentaries that resist the impulse toward narrative.

The Setup

At the beginning of every documentary is the setup, which frames a central question or "problem" for the audience. This establishes the narrative expectations and makes possible a sense of closure at the end of the film when a solution or answer is revealed.

Television documentaries and reality shows often accomplish this in exceedingly direct terms and with remarkable economy, as when Gordon Ramsey tells the chefs on the second episode of Season 17 of *Hell's Kitchen*, "The chef that creates the best bar menu item will be featured on the Hell's Kitchen Bar Menu throughout the season . . . and will be safe from tonight's elimination. Make two plates—you've got forty minutes." The goal, stakes, and rules for the entire show have been stipulated in the first thirty-five seconds of its running time.

HGTV is an entire network of shows devoted to problematic houses and dreamy remodeling solutions, as on the show *Pool Kings*, which features makeovers of backyard swimming pools. A typical episode begins with a list of issues that the remodel needs to solve. "Our current pool is a mess; it's a nightmare," says homeowner Lisa in

Figure 3.1   One of the many problems in need of a solution on *Pool Kings*

an episode titled "The Pirate Treasure Pool" from Season 1. "It's really not functional for young kids," chimes in her husband Mike. They follow with a quick list of three attributes they expect from the dream remodel, which are helpfully put onscreen in wish-list graphics that read, "Large patio," "Modern Style," and "Block highway noise" (see figure 3.1). "Most important about this pool," concludes Lisa, "is we want to be the spot where everybody's coming to play."

The episode then goes on to blast through a host of other problem/solution vignettes, including where to stage the construction materials, how to build a waterfall feature that is perfectly straight ("or else we'll have to tear it all apart and start over"), and what to do about a ruptured water line after the crew inadvertently slices through it during demolition. All of these problems have subproblems and solutions of their own. ("To turn the water off we have to get in the garage, [but] the garage is locked, and the owners are out of town so we have to get ahold of someone somehow to get in there!") Each problem has a solution, and the enduring popularity of these shows is surely due in part to their reassuring messages of narrative completion, which they reliably deliver by the dozen in each show. At the end of this episode, the pool is presented as a masterpiece that will surely bring the neighborhood out to play.[3]

Figure 3.2 The artist Maleonn in *Our Time Machine*

Feature documentaries often take more time to set up the "problem," and may do so in more subtle terms. The opening minutes of S. Leo Chiang and Yang Sun's *Our Time Machine* is loaded with subtle provocations, each of which is designed to provoke curiosity about what the "problem" will be (see Figure 3.2).

- A title card with a quotation from H. G. Wells that reads, "We all have our time machines, don't we?" (*What is the significance of the quote? What is the "time machine" in this film?*)
- An image of a sonogram of a baby in utero as the audience hears a voice that states, "Dear child, how should I introduce you to this world?" (*Whose child is this?*)
- An animated segment of shadow play against an illuminated screen. (*Why shadows and puppets? How is this related to the overall story?*)
- The main title: "Our Time Machine." (*Amplifies the question posed by the H. G. Wells quotation.*)
- A scene of the Chinese artist Maleonn painting a watercolor of a father and son while saying in voice-over, "Dear child, there comes a moment when we must grow up. We suddenly realize that forever does not exist in this world." (*Maleonn is identified as the father of the baby in the sonogram, but a new theme of mortality is introduced; what does it portend?*)

- Maleonn experiments in his home studio with shadow play. (*The question of "why shadows and puppets" is answered, but the main "problem" remains opaque.*)

After the audience sees more of Maleonn's extraordinary art work and learns that his father is becoming senile, a scene arrives that clarifies the problem. As Maleonn sits for a radio interview, he explains his next project: "Our play has two main characters: the father and the son. The father is losing his memory, and the son is sad to see him confused. The son builds a time machine so he can bring the father back to his childhood when he was five or ten [so they can] go back again and again to revisit moments in their lives." This statement gives meaning to the previous scenes and delivers a clearly presented problem: the son must finish work on the autobiographical play before the father's memory makes it impossible for him to comprehend it. The rest of the film will elaborate on the development and eventual resolution of this issue.

Whether the "problem" statement comes at the end of a carefully laid patchwork of insinuations (as in *Our Time Machine)* or accomplished more coarsely and succinctly (as on *Pool Kings)*, a great majority of documentaries announce their "problem statement" quite early. Watch any feature documentary and you can usually find it.

- At two and a half minutes into Julie Shaw's 2003 television documentary *Living with Michael Jackson*, host Martin Bashir delivers the first narration of the film, which neatly sums up the premise: "Eight months ago, I put a proposal to Michael Jackson: 'Show me the real man, but show me everything; put nothing off-limits.' He thought about it and then he said, 'Yes, come to Neverland.'"
- In the opening sequence of Susan Lacy's *Jane Fonda in Five Acts,* a brief archival montage builds up Jane Fonda's bona fides as a superstar, a highly controversial public figure, and a woman of polar opposites—a sex kitten who campaigns for feminist causes, an anticorporate crusader who marries billionaire CNN founder Ted Turner. Taking up the mantle of

this last characterization, an interviewer asks her, "You turn around and marry a billionaire. How do you go from one [extreme] to the other without completely losing yourself in there somewhere?" The audience meanwhile sees starkly contrasting pictures of Fonda, appearing shy and self-conscious in some, supremely self-confident in others. The main title comes up: *Jane Fonda in Five Acts*, and the question has been implicitly posed: who is the real Jane Fonda?

- At five and a half minutes into Robert Greene's film *Actress*, actress Brandy Burre (*The Wire*) sits in the kids' playroom of her Hudson Valley home and states glumly, "I moved to Beacon. I'm not acting. So this is my creative outlet, I guess." She gestures half-heartedly to her kids' things, then unexpectedly repeats the sentence verbatim a second time as if she's giving the director the option of a second take.[4] The double-pronged message—she is genuinely unhappy in her real-life role as a housewife and is also hyperaware of her status as a character in Greene's film—kicks off the duality that the film will play with for the rest of its ninety-minute running time: *Actress* will play as both a real-life drama (will she find happiness?) and a self-aware meta-analysis of the nature of performance in documentary.

Position

In any narrative, the meaning of a moment is produced in part by what position it occupies. A scene in which a participant says, "I'm not going to be satisfied until we've run every one of these scam artists out of town" can function as the setup for a documentary (defining the "problem" or goal of the protagonist) if it is placed near the beginning, regardless of whether it was actually uttered near the start of filming. Ditto for scenes that make great endings. A statement serving as a witty coda is meaningful in large part because of its status as the concluding remark and becomes meaningful because it refers back to previous moments, not simply for the raw content it contains.

A good example of this can be found in the conclusion of the Jehane Noujaim / Chris Hegedus film *Startup.com*, an entertaining chronicle of the rise and fall of a startup internet venture in the late 1990s. In the film's final montage, the audience sees entrepreneur Tom Herman playing guitar with his daughter while Kaleil Tuzman, his business partner, is seen driving somewhere with a dog in the front seat beside him. In the final shots, Kaleil is seen eating ramen noodles beside an unidentified woman who looks offscreen at the dog. The woman goes outside, picks up a bone, and throws it to the dog, which runs after it (Figure 3.3).

The sequence is nearly meaningless on its own. *Who is the woman? What does the dog have to do with anything? What is Tom doing?* Yet because of its status as a concluding moment, the images are imbued with meanings that they otherwise would not have. In two earlier scenes, Kaleil's girlfriend at the time (a different woman) complained

Figure 3.3 An unnamed woman throws a dog a bone in *Startup.com*

that he did not spend enough time with her, and mentioned that she was unhappy that he resisted her entreaties to adopt a puppy together. By the end of the film, Kaleil's unhealthy workaholic tendencies have scuttled not only the adoption but also the relationship. Tom has similarly plunged himself so deeply into work that his relationship with his young daughter has suffered. Thus, the meaning of the sequence is crystal clear: both men have grown, and each has come out the other end of a harrowing life journey having learned a lesson. Tom is spending more time with his daughter, and Kaleil is taking a step toward a positive work/life balance by engaging in the give-and-take of a healthy relationship with a new partner. The scene would have been jarring used anywhere else in the film, but in this context it functions as a kind of coda, working almost purely on the level of subtext.

The Crisis Moment

If a standard narrative requires compelling conflict and increasing levels of narrative tension, concluding with a dramatic climax, how can this be created given the fundamental mundanity of everyday life? One time-tested approach involves the filmmaker inserting themself into a situation that already has preexisting conflict and a firmly established endpoint. Robert Drew, a documentary producer from the 1960s who worked with filmmakers such as Albert Maysles, D. A. Pennebaker, Ricky Leacock, and Hope Ryden, was an innovator in this respect and described his approach thusly:

> What makes us different from other reporting, and from other documentary filmmaking, is that in each of these stories there is a time when a [person] comes against moments of tension, and pressure, and revelation, and decision. It's these moments that interest us most.[5]

Drew focused on finding individuals in stressful situations who would show their "true colors" in moments of crisis, thus supposedly revealing their inner character. His choice of subject matter is telling:

- *Mooney vs. Fowle* (high school football coaches prepare their teams for a showdown)
- *The Chair* (a Chicago attorney hurries to obtain a stay of execution for his client)
- *Jane* (Jane Fonda prepares for the biggest theater role of her career)
- *On the Pole* (auto racer Eddie Sachs prepares for the Indianapolis 500)
- *Susan Starr* (A talented young concert pianist prepares for the biggest competition of her life)
- *Primary* (John F. Kennedy and Hubert Humphrey duke it out in Wisconsin as they fight to win the Democratic primary nomination for president)

In these and other Drew Associates films, the filmmakers put up shop in a preexisting contest of some kind, be it a political race, a sporting event, or the preparation for the opening day of a performance. The shooting period is limited, with a built-in conclusion and a protagonist under pressure to achieve a particular outcome. The excitement as Drew saw it was watching drama play out in real time; thus he eschewed interviews and focused on verité shooting. To Drew, this arrangement created the ideal conditions for the kind of storytelling he wanted to pursue. "The story for me has to go someplace; something has to happen," he said. "What really happens in any of these stories is that something is revealed about the people."

It bears mentioning that Drew's approach carries some questionable assumptions. Is the crisis moment really the one that is most revealing of "true character"? Perhaps a verité moment that takes place weeks later, once the protagonists have had time to digest their victory or defeat, would be more telling. Perhaps the passivity of the observational approach would miss the deeper psychological details of the situation that would have been uncovered via a particularly trenchant question from an interviewer.[6] And what kind of truth is really revealed when we consider the fact that performers, sports figures, and politicians are individuals who are adept at choosing exactly what to show the camera and what to conceal?

Despite these questions, the importance of Drew's central innovation of finding "crisis moments" and exploiting them for documentary drama cannot be understated. Indeed, reality television is just a logical extension of this format as it discards the need to find subjects already engaged in a real-life contest and simply creates one of its own making. This leaves the producers fully in control of every aspect of the shooting environment, from the nature and development of the contest (including changing the rules midstream to engineer more drama), to the casting of the participants (including some who are chosen because they are likely to stir up trouble or because they are emotionally fragile), to the location itself (including cameras, hidden and otherwise, placed in a variety of locations.)

The "contest" documentary, popular in the last few decades, is another prime example of this. Films like *Spellbound* (about the national spelling bee), *First Position* (about the Youth America Grand Prix ballet competition), *Science Fair* (about the International Science and Engineering Fair), and the much-celebrated 1997 film *Hands on a Hard Body* (about a contest awarding a new truck to whichever individual can keep a hand continually touching the body of the vehicle) all work backward from an end point at which a winner will be crowned champion, documenting the joys and heartbreaks of what happens along the way.

Producing the Narrative Turn

A fascinating hybrid of the traditional "crisis moment" documentary and reality television is the A&E show *Intervention*, which has run for over twenty seasons since its premiere in March 2005. The inner workings of its production, discussed for the first time here by its onetime executive producer Dan Partland, reveal fascinating insights into fundamental storytelling conventions on unscripted television shows, and by extension into many documentary conventions more generally.

On the show, viewers are introduced to individuals with extreme addiction issues who have come to the end of their rope. They are usually addicted to drugs or alcohol, but the show has also featured gambling addiction, video game addiction, sex addiction, plastic surgery addiction, and anorexic and bulimic behaviors. Over the course of a forty-six-minute running time, the audience sees the protagonist engaging in this addiction in verité footage, learns about its psychological roots in the family dynamic via interviews with family members and close friends, observes a preintervention session with the family run by a professional addiction specialist, and finally witnesses the intervention itself. The addicts are confronted with a choice: accept the offer of a fully paid in-patient treatment program or have their closest loved ones cut all ties with them forever (see Figure 3.4)—an intervention method pioneered by the Episcopal priest Vernon Johnson.

If this sounds salacious, you are not wrong. The voice-over artist who reads the opening "adult content" warning does it in a breathy, teasing voice that positively dares the audience to watch (*"viewer discretion advised!"*), and much of what is shown is indeed highly personal and upsetting. Yet it should be noted that interventions carried out according to the Johnson model, whether recorded or not, include the threat of severing all contact, which may be necessary to save the life of the addict.[7] While addiction specialists differ on whether this

Figure 3.4 An intervention on *Intervention*

model is the most effective, the show is quite realistic in its portrayal of how such an intervention is carried out and of the behaviors commonly exhibited by those with hardcore addictions.

Thus the show finds a preexisting situation (the protagonist living with an addiction) and actively brings it to a conclusion through a process that is artificial in some respects since it would not have occurred without the participation of the filmmaker, and organic in others since it is carried out in much the same way it would be if the families had engaged the services of a professional interventionist themselves.

Partland, who was executive producer of 150 episodes of the show between and 2007 2011, describes how the show was broken up methodically into a five-act structure (with a commercial break between each act).

> The first act was character introduction, establishing what we called the quantification—quantifying the extent of the problem—as well as the backstory of how they got there. We wanted exposition, character, and backstory, at the end of which we would flip back to present tense.
>
> Act 2 was what we called the complicating factors in the present. It had two pods in it that were supposed to highlight the most important conflicts that existed in the addict's life. It could be a bit of backstory that we held back from Act 1 that made it particularly hard to get the addict out of their addiction, or it could be a detail of the family dynamic.
>
> Act 3 would bring the conflict to a head with whatever the most urgent problem was that they were having. And then in the middle of Act 3, the interventionist would be introduced and would do a preintervention where the family members would be told to produce letters to read at the intervention.
>
> Act 4 was the intervention, when everything came together. The family members read their letters and the addict wrestled with whether or not they were going to accept the offer of treatment. They usually did agree, and we showed them leaving for their trip to the treatment center.
>
> Act 5 showed their reunion with their families a couple months later with them talking about what had changed.

The production of the show was methodical, and after helming dozens of episodes Partland had honed the operation into a well-oiled machine built around producing what he referred to as *characterological turns*, which are the crucial moments when characters develop in an important way by making a transformation in their lives or discovering something about their addiction pattern.

> The whole goal was character development, so when we evaluated which stories to pick, one of the key things we were looking for was, what are the potential turns for this addict and also for their closest loved ones? There should be something for the mom to learn and something for the dad to learn, and hopefully there's something for the siblings. And we would go out to shoot it with at least one or two turns in mind for just about everybody. What was their blind spot? What weren't they seeing in this thing?

This would start with extensive preproduction phone interviews. By interviewing all the main players with the same rigor that an investigative journalist would bring to a news story, the producers could identify key tensions, family dynamics, and bits of family history that could provide a credible psychological backstory for the addict and insights about the roots of the problem. This research gave the producer a road map for what to document throughout the intense three-week production schedule, which started with verité shooting, was followed by lengthy interviews, and concluded with the intervention.

> Let's say we learned in preproduction that the mom and the daughter [the one with the addiction] had a fraught relationship. Mom was competitive with her and never really showed love. We've preproduced and we know what the conflicts are; we just want to see them on their feet and let them happen organically in the verité shooting. So when the daughter asks, "Will you pass me the remote?" while they're watching TV, and the mother says, "No, no, we're going to watch my show," you can join that with the interview material you know you're going to get and make that stand in for "Mom always came first." The audience will

understand why the addict is incensed that mom won't give her the remote. We always wanted big material, but if we didn't *have* big material, we could make it *feel* big emotionally if the audience really understood the nature of the conflict.

The ideal scenario from the production's point of view would be for the cameras to arrive just in time for the loved ones to realize their complicity as enablers in the self-destructive behavior, and to show that discovery on camera. In producing the show, however, Partland bumped into a truism of documentary filmmaking, which is that the filmmakers' interaction with the participants can actually *produce* changes in their lives. The preinterview is undoubtedly a form of talk therapy, with the producer asking intimate, probing questions, spending long amounts of time listening, and thus inviting self-reflection. Because of this, sometimes the production team would observe that the subjects would start to "turn" before they had arrived with their cameras.

We had to be careful in the preproduction because we didn't want them to have wrestled with their thoughts so much that they had started realizing their blind spots ahead of schedule. We wanted them to develop, but we needed to capture it on camera.

The interviews were exhaustive—often five hours apiece—with all the key players. Unlike most documentary productions, followup interviews were not considered a viable option because "once the intervention happened, the status quo of everyone's relationships was so fundamentally shifted that there was no going back," says Partland. "You had to get everything, and you had just one shot at it."

While the *Intervention* model may seem formulaic, it is not fundamentally different from the structure followed in many other feature documentaries. Amy Ziering, producer of such celebrated investigative documentaries as *The Hunting Ground*, *The Invisible War*, and *On the Record*, says, "We really do cleave to classic narrative film structure. We look at arc; we look at character; we look at three- to five-act structures; and we are sure we are hitting certain beats."

Those beats in her films often include cathartic moments in which survivors confront various kinds of trauma by saying it aloud and coming forward with their stories. In the case of *The Invisible War* and *The Hunting Ground*, which deal with painful cases of sexual assault that have been kept quiet, the act of sitting for the documentary interview becomes a cathartic, healing moment all by itself. Ziering, known for producing moments of extraordinary intimacy with her interview subjects, understands the therapeutic nature of the encounter.

> I tell every subject, "Your mental health comes first. If you decide you don't want to answer a question, that's fine. If you want us to leave, that's fine. If we have to stop, that's fine. You're in control here." And then I do a very long interview. I don't have a clipboard, and I'm not looking at questions; it's just a conversation. It's not rushed, it's very thoughtful. At the end, I always make sure to ask, "Is there anything I didn't ask that you want to say?" All of this creates a very, very safe space.
>
> When we interviewed Corey [Cioca; see Figure 3.5] for *The Invisible War*, at one point she started to cry. We stopped the interview and I gave her a hug and said, "You don't have to relive the past right now if you

Figure 3.5 Corey Cioca's interview in *The Invisible War*

don't want. You're here with us now and it's safe." And she said that this totally changed her perspective on her experience, because no one had ever said that to her before. She had been sort of trapped, and it was an epiphany for her. I often get letters that say, "Even though you didn't put my interview in your film, just being able to talk to you was really important. No one had believed in me before and just to be heard made all the difference."

Cathartic moments are a staple of many documentaries, and documentary filmmakers are always in search of them. It should not be surprising to find that by carrying out an essentially therapeutic role in their relationships with the participants, filmmakers end up *producing* these moments in addition to just observing them.

No recent documentary has done this more explicitly than Robert Greene's *Procession*, which enlisted drama therapist Monica Phinney to work with the film's participants, all survivors of sexual abuse by Catholic priests in Kansas City, to create short film reenactments of their experience. The therapist and the costs of production were all borne by the filmmakers, who documented the process and wove the footage into a dramatic arc. What's fascinating here is just how explicitly the men's emancipation from their trauma was tied to the constructs of narrative that this chapter has sought to reveal. As the film progresses, survivor after survivor travels to the actual site of their abuse so that they can confront their memories head-on. Yet when Dan Laurine tries to find the exact lake house where he was abused over thirty years prior, they reach a dead end; he has no leads to follow, and there are too many possible houses on Lake Viking to pin down the actual location. At one crucial moment, fellow survivor Michael Sandridge says to him, "I feel bad because there's no ending for you yet, Dan . . . I think Joe will have an ending, maybe Ed will, I don't know. I'd like to see you have an ending." In this film, every character's catharsis is tied explicitly to narrative closure, and the creation of a new story (via the staged reenactments) is necessary for the emancipation from the narratives of the past.

Producing the Narrative Turn with Juxtaposition

Producing narrative turns is also possible via means of pure juxtaposition. When editing *Precious Knowledge*, I worked with director Ari Palos and producer Eren Isabel McGinnis to build problem/solution vignettes into a complex story about an ethnic studies program in the Tucson public schools that was shut down in a conflict over its content. The political battle over the program, which had been created to close the achievement gap between Latinx youth and their white counterparts, was interesting; but without personalizing the achievement gap by showing the stories of particular students, the issue might have seemed dry and abstract.

In the film's opening segment, student Pricila talks about the emotional devastation of having her father deported to Mexico, Crystal discusses the burden of having to take care of her younger siblings, and Gilbert recounts losing many friends to gang violence and a punitive criminal justice system. In isolation, these stories seemed unrelated to the problem of Latinx student achievement; but with additional words about how each student was having trouble in school, the film implies a causal relationship between their life circumstances and their poor educational achievement.

Once this was set up, the narrative builds their stories as living embodiments of the larger problem of Latinx achievement. The audience sees each of the three characters on their way to school— Crystal driving her truck, Gilbert driving his car, and Pricila taking the bus (see Figures 3.6–3.8). Again, these shots themselves are neutral—they have neither smiles nor frowns on their faces, and they're engaging in an utterly mundane task, but the placement of the shots in juxtaposition with one of the administrators talking about the enormity of the task before them ("approximately 50 percent of Hispanics drop out of school, and the numbers . . . are getting worse") turns them into powerful symbols: test subjects for the new curriculum that may—or may not—bring transformation. The fact that they all are filmed seeming to travel the same direction (seated screen left, looking screen right) completes the visual metaphor.

Figures 3.6–3.8 Crystal, Gilbert, and Pricila on their way to school in *Precious Knowledge*

As the film progresses, the audience is presented with three very short scenes in which some small narrative "turn" occurs for each student. Crystal, who was previously withdrawn and shy in class, gives a successful presentation as her mom talks about the vast improvement she has seen in her daughter's grades. Gilbert is seen talking animatedly about his interest in the reading material in one of his classes over shots of him sitting in the same class, listening intently. And in Pricila's case, the audience sees something seemingly insignificant occur: she smiles. While her in-class behavior to this point had shown her to be serious and buttoned up, the film shows one particular moment in which her teacher tells a joke and she cracks a smile in response. This tiny problem/solution vignette, accompanied by voice-over of her teacher talking about how he uses humor to get through to some of the tougher students, stands for something much larger than its literal meaning: Pricila has found a connection to her teacher and is now achieving like never before. The fact that this was borne out by objective measures of grade improvement and test results was crucial, but it would have had no *cinematic* meaning without these small moments of transformation that the audience witnessed.

The idea of progression and causality need not work in only one direction. Flashbacks can create a turn by suddenly building a "before/after" dynamic with the addition of a new piece of information that builds backstory. This has rarely been done with more economy or simplicity than in the first episode of Season 1 of *Couples Therapy*, the Showtime documentary series in which the audience witnesses several couples go through multiple sessions of couples therapy to try to work out their issues. The audience is introduced to Evelyn and Alan in the first episode and told in a title card that they are "three months into therapy." At the end of a tearful session in which Alan expresses exasperation that "nothing will make her happy" and Evelyn seethes with anger at his indifference to her concerns, they reveal that they are ready to call it quits on their marriage. Orna, the therapist, takes this in silently and bids them an awkward farewell. In the next scene the audience sees the same couple in the waiting room again. Their body language is completely different: they are warm and relaxed with each other, radiating affection. As they greet Orna's dog with broad smiles, a devastating title card appears on the screen: "THREE MONTHS EARLIER." In this single title card, the audience instantly sees that three months of therapy seem to have exposed deep faults in their mutual trust, and that they may not belong together. Rarely has there been a more succinct example of how the narrative turn—a difference or progression between point A and point B—creates a feeling of narrative development.

Micronarratives

When discussing narrative, attention is usually focused on the big picture: how does a story build and evolve over the course of a ninety-minute feature or a thirty- or sixty-minute television show? But narrative is at play on a micro level as well; it is woven into the fabric of every single scene and can often play out over the course of a single shot.

For inspiration, let's look at an example from the Showtime limited series *Escape at Dannemora*, a scripted retelling of the 2015 prison escape and subsequent manhunt of David Sweat and Richard Matt that occurred in upstate New York in 2015. As Sweat (Paul Dano) exits the bathroom of a deserted cabin with a gun he has just found tucked into his belt near the small of his back, the sound of a second gun being cocked is heard offscreen. This sound is the start of the micronarrative, because it instantly triggers a question in the minds of the audience members: Where did the sound come from? The show now has the choice about how long to draw out the drama before the question is answered. In this case, instead of quickly satisfying the audience's curiosity by cutting straight to the source of the sound (which would decrease the narrative tension) the show deliciously draws out the moment of discovery. The camera lingers on Dano and follows him as he walks slowly across the room to his fellow escapee Richard Matt (Benicio del Toro). Only once Dano reaches del Toro does the audience see del Toro turning to say, "Look what I found," as he blows into the barrel of a shotgun to dust it off. Del Toro has found a gun of his own in the cabin, and the two escapees now eye each other suspiciously.

The same question-and-answer pattern can be found at multiple moments in every documentary. Often it lasts for only two or three seconds, as in a scene from Stanley Nelson's *Attica*, which tells the story of the shocking slaughter of dozens of inmates of color in a standoff at Attica Prison in 1971. Former prisoners have just finished describing the moment when they had the upper hand in the riot that set off the conflict, and then the face of a white man appears on the screen in a family snapshot. There is a subtle pause to allow the provocation to trigger curiosity in the audience: *Who is this guy?* Two and a half seconds later, a woman's voice is heard describing the man as an Attica prison guard and the film then cuts to her to let her continue the story.

This may seem unremarkable but consider the alternative: the film cuts directly to the woman, who immediately starts talking about her father as the film then cuts to his picture to identify him. In this scenario the same information has been conveyed but the audience has not been engaged in the same way. There has been no narrative provocation, and they have not been led through a question-and-answer progression that briefly forestalled narrative completion. From this example we can see that narrative works not only on the level of juicy story development and plot twists, but also in the very fabric of information delivery.

Callbacks

Another narrative device in documentaries is the callback. The callback is a moment in a documentary when a new piece of information is introduced that sheds light on a previous scene, thus calling that scene up in the mind of the viewer. It's the "aha" moment when a revelation occurs and makes the audience reevaluate what they've been told thus far. *Three Identical Strangers* has at least five such callbacks, and much of the narrative structure is built around them. It presents a structure wherein the core story is told, and then new circles of information are added, each of which calls back to the original depiction to ask the audience to reevaluate it.

The film begins with an entertaining telling of how identical triplet brothers, separated at birth, rediscover each other. When Bobby shows up for his freshman year at college and everyone seems to recognize him, he tracks down his brother David (who attends the same school) and both are shocked and delighted at their newfound discovery. The third brother Eddy watches a TV news story about the other two, and the shock and delight is repeated all over again when they meet. The three become instantly bonded, moving in with each other and doing almost everything together. They take on New York City, open a restaurant together, and seem to find new meaning in their lives. Along the way, it is casually mentioned that two of the brothers had been adopted via the Louise Wise Services Adoption Agency.

At this point, author Lawrence Wright is introduced, and within one minute he explains his long-standing research into the subject of identical twins. As the pacing slows down and the music adds an element of foreboding and mystery, he utters the following words:

> In the process of my research I came across this obscure scientific article. It referenced this secret study in which identical siblings had been separated. I was shocked and intrigued.

Given the context, it is clear by the time we hear "identical siblings had been separated" that these three men must have been part of this study. But the film continues to nail down the association as Wright makes his accusation in the plainest language possible: "They were separating identical babies at birth for the purpose of this scientific experiment, and these babies had all come from one adoption agency in New York City."

From the perspective of narrative clarity, the job is complete. But from a storytelling point of view, it's possible to cash in and create a dramatic moment by making the audience reevaluate old footage in light of new revelations. What follows is a forty-second montage in which fragments from a variety of previous scenes ("Were you adopted?" "Twins separated at birth . . ." "All of us were adopted from Louise Wise") are stitched together with music at a steadily accelerating tempo, ending on a shot of an archival photo of a nameplate that reads "Louise Wise Services" (see Figure 3.9).[8]

Some of what's happening here is also "insurance." Nonfiction content creators know that there can be a large variation in the rates at which their audiences arrive at each point of meaning recognition, and that some need more handholding than others to get the point. In this respect the film has much in common with television documentaries, which tend to be more didactic than films and explicitly nail down every aspect of their intended meaning, leaving nothing to chance.

Perhaps no show is more shameless in this respect than *The Bachelor*, where belaboring the point has reached a form of high art. By playing and replaying the action of a single scene repeatedly and explaining in voice-over what is already obvious from verité, *The Bachelor* manages to pad out each week of its slim narrative into 90- and 120-minute epics. In the teaser at the opening of the fourth episode of Season 24, Alayah, who had been sent packing by bachelor Peter in the previous episode, shows up unannounced at one of the cocktail parties and asks to speak with him. Four women react to her

Figure 3.9 An archival photo in *Three Identical Strangers*

arrival with open-mouthed awe. "Shut the front door!" they exclaim in unison, creating a self-censored version of "Shut the fuck up!" Cut to the shocked faces of Sydney and Kiarra as the audience hears one woman say, "Why is Alayah here?" and another opine, "That was so disrespectful to all of us, it was a slap in the face."

The teaser has thus spilled the beans about the "shocking" incident at the outset of the episode, but later in the show it is reprised when it plays out in full.[9] The shock and awe from the women are stretched out much as an explosion in an action film is repeated several times in quick succession to elongate its impact.

> "Shut the front door!" they say in unison.
>
> "Wait, what!?!?" says Kiarra.
>
> "What is happening!?" says Mykenna.
>
> "There's a ghost in the room!" remarks Savannah.
>
> "What? Wait!" exclaims someone else.
>
> As Alayah continues to stride toward Peter, who's having a chat with another contestant, the audience continues to hear reactions.
>
> "The ghost of Alayah just walked in," says Savannah.
>
> "Last week Alayah went home, and so every single one of us, our jaws dropped," says Mykenna, describing what the audience has already seen twice over.
>
> "What?!" says one.
>
> "What?!" says another.
>
> "What the [bleeped expletive]?" says a third.
>
> "What's she doing here?" says a fourth.
>
> Tammy, a woman that the show consistently turns to for hyperbolic interview quotes, says, "Everyone is shooketh to the core!"

Incredibly, the scene is still not over. After showing Peter's reaction to the unexpected arrival, the show cuts to Tammy in interview again, who summarizes the entire scene one last time: "Last week at the pool party Peter thought it was necessary to send Alayah home. But now Alayah's back, and I have no idea what's going on." A scene that took perhaps ten seconds to play out in real time has been elongated to an incredible two minutes and fifteen seconds.

Non-narrative Documentaries

This chapter would not be complete without a giant caveat: not all documentaries are driven by narrative. Though they tend to lurk online outside the orbit of the major streamers and are not well-known outside of academia and the art world, there are numerous documentaries whose concerns lie largely outside of the realm of traditional storytelling. "Immersive" or "transcendental" documentaries, whose purpose is to build a satisfying aesthetic experience rather than to satisfy a desire to "see how it turns out," announce their intentions differently. By pointedly *not* posing a specific narrative question at the outset but instead setting up aesthetic or tonal patterns, these films nonetheless answer the question "What is this documentary about?" for the audience. The 2012 documentary *Leviathan*, for instance, begins with a shot over eight minutes in length from a GoPro camera mounted on the helmet of one of the fishing crew aboard a nighttime vessel on rough seas. The sounds of the machinery are harsh and violent; the ultrawide angle of the camera gives a sense of motion and depth that makes the activities feel dangerous and exciting. The picture is extremely high contrast, so that there are large pools of inky black in almost every frame. The film speaks: *there will be no big narrative payoff; the extraordinary sights and sounds are the point.* Indeed, this turns out to be accurate; the audience is not even shown a close-up of any member of the fishing crew until almost thirty minutes into the film, something that would never occur in a more narratively driven documentary.[10] Notably, these films also tend to have little dialogue and no narration. The online manifesto for the Harvard University Sensory Ethnography Lab, a major player in the movement for this strand of documentary filmmaking, is explicit about its disinterest in dialogue and narration, claiming that the Lab "encourages attention to the many dimensions of the world, both animate and inanimate, that may only with difficulty, if at all, be rendered with words."[11]

Also consider the oeuvre of James Benning, a documentary filmmaker whose five-decade career has been an experiment in challenging audiences to reorient their narrative-heavy ways of seeing.

Sometimes dubbed a "structuralist" filmmaker, Benning's films are often organized not around a central character or even a single location, but by the structure of the edit. For example, each of the three films in his *California Trilogy*—*El Valley Centro*, *Los*, and *Sogobi*—features thirty-five lockdown shots that are exactly two and a half minutes in length each. *El Valley Centro* is a portrait of the California Central Valley featuring shots of farmland, reservoirs, trains, and the occasional lonely road; *Los* features urban Los Angeles cityscapes; *Sogobi* is concerned with nature vistas across the state. Without humans (or even animals) occupying the role of central protagonist, what organizes the logic of the shots? One might imagine each starting with birds chirping in the morning and dusk setting in the evening, but there is no obvious chronological order either. Instead, Benning seems more interested in pure rhythm. In one shot from *El Valley Centro*, industrial sprinklers rotate 360 degrees with their rhythmic *thp, thp, thp, thp, thp*, watering a giant agricultural field, and drops of water fall near the camera once per revolution. In another, a small aircraft makes low-flying passes over a huge field of crops, coming and going with regularity as it sprays pesticide (Figure 3.10).

Figure 3.10 *El Valley Centro*

One finds oneself forced into observing the most minute details and patterns of life, as the film offers the passage of time itself as worthy of attention instead of what an event portends or what question it will answer. In *BNSF*, his longest film, a single static shot plays out for well over three hours showing a rural landscape with a single set of train tracks slicing through the landscape on the left of the frame. About every twenty minutes, a train approaches from the lower left of the frame and chugs on its bent arc to its exit in the upper left. The rhythms here are extremely long, and patience is required (the Australian avant-jazz group The Necks, with their sustained silences, is a possible musical equivalent.) But as the film goes on, the train's arrivals seem to get more imposing, more insistent, more violent. Is the train actually getting louder or is it just one's increasing awareness of its presence?

The films of Wang Bing offer another way of thinking about story. In his film *Bitter Money*, we accompany three individuals from a small Chinese village on a long train ride to a large, unnamed textile city and then witness scenes of their lives as they negotiate a daily existence of twelve-hour workdays and cramped sleeping quarters. The scenes are long and unhurried, such that the train ride alone contains a single shot of two minutes in length composed of nothing but sleeping passengers. Instead of posing the question *what will happen to these people?* the intention seems to be *look at what is happening to these people.* As the film progresses it introduces vignettes with a whole constellation of other characters trying to eke out a living in the garment sweatshops, and the narrative becomes a collective one. At the end, one man (whom the audience has never seen before and does not see again) leaves frustrated and brokenhearted, fired by his boss after being told that he was too slow, while a woman gets her payday and buys some of the garments that she herself sewed, not overjoyed but satisfied enough. Even without a central character to attach a story to, a question has still been obliquely asked and answered via a mosaic of loosely related protagonists who all negotiate the same system. As we have seen, narrative may operate at multiple levels and in highly varied ways as a documentary progresses through its running time.

Notes

1. Hayden White, "The Value of Narrativity in the Representation of Reality." *Critical Inquiry* 7, no. 1 (1980): 5–27.
2. Becker refers to the work of USC emeritus professor of communication Walter R. Fisher, who argued for a narrative approach to rhetoric and communication theory. Becker is here quoted from a draft book manuscript titled *The Frankenbite: Ethics and Reality in Factual Programming*. The finished version of the excellent book is titled *Creating Reality in Factual Television: The Frankenbite and Other Fakes* (London: Routledge, 2020).
3. There is a strong subtext of wish fulfillment in many home improvement shows like this one. While the ostensible drama is about the renovation of this particular pool, the underlying message invites the audience to ogle the material wealth of the homeowners and envy their ability to spend massive amounts of money on discretionary items like this.
4. *Actress*, directed by Robert Greene (4th Row Films, 2014), 00:06:00.
5. Alan Rosenthal, *New Challenges for Documentary* (Berkeley: University of California Press: 1988), 274.
6. Some of these questions were posed in a different formulation by Steven Mamber in the chapter "Direct Cinema and the Crisis Structure" in his book *Cinema Verité in America: Studies in Uncontrolled Documentary* (Cambridge, MA: MIT Press, 1974).
7. Doug Wintemute, "The Disturbing Untold Truth of Intervention," *Nicki Swift*, August 28, 2018, https://www.nickiswift.com/132199/the-disturbing-untold-truth-of-intervention/.
8. *Three Identical Strangers*, directed by Tim Wardle (RAW TV, 2018), 00:24:16.
9. *The Bachelor*, Season 24, Episode 4, created by Mike Fleiss (ABC), 00:33:40.
10. Reviews of *Leviathan* on the Kanopy website show a range of responses to the bold choices taken in the film. Some viewers raved about it ("This movie SLAMS"), while viewers expecting something more conventional did not see the point ("Wow, there's an hour and a half you'll never get back").
11. Harvard Sensory Ethnography Lab website, https://sel.fas.harvard.edu/.

4

Presence Framing

As we noted in the introduction, fiction films create a world that is understood to reside in the realm of the imaginary. Fiction films "are experiences of magical observation, defying ordinary physical limits and forms of accountability," observes David MacDougall.[1] The audience gets total access to the characters, showing them from cameras mounted on the ceilings in their bedrooms, swooping left and right of them as they walk down the street, and happening to show up at precisely the right moment to catch the emotional apex of every scene in a pristine close-up. Even unflashy fiction films that play as stylistically realist still usually posit the camera as an unacknowledged, invisible observer.

This conceit becomes complicated in a documentary. Since the camera was rolling during moments of real life rather than on a film set, the audience may be more attuned to the camera's presence, and that presence creates a burden for the filmmaker. *This actually happened*, the audience is reminded. *What I'm seeing really took place and a camera was there to record it.* In response, every documentary develops a strategy for presenting the putative relationship between the filmmaker, the camera, and the subjects. I call this the framing of presence, or *presence framing*.[2] It may present the camera as an uncomplicated window onto the world, which does not notice its presence, or as an instrument for interaction and provocation, or as a potentially dangerous tool in need of critique and disruption. The camera may even be referenced by the subjects and seem to recognize its own existence, but as we will see, this too is a frame.[3]

Frames are a concept that gained currency in the early years of artificial intelligence research with the release of MIT researcher

How Documentaries Work. Jacob Bricca, Oxford University Press. © Oxford University Press 2023.
DOI: 10.1093/oso/9780197554104.003.0005

Marvin Minsky's 1974 article "A Framework for Representing Knowledge." Seeking to understand the practicalities of how human intelligence works, Minsky posited that "when one encounters a new situation . . . one selects from memory a structure called a Frame." These frames, according to Veerle Ros et al., "can be understood as sets of expectations that we may project onto a situation . . . in order to make sense of it."[4] When one walks up to a checkout counter at a department store, for instance, a stereotyped understanding of the encounter informs what we expect to occur and how we choose to act. "Attached to each frame are several kinds of information," wrote Minsky. "Some of this information is about how to use the frame. Some is about what one can expect to happen next. Some is about what to do if these expectations are not confirmed."[5]

In the case of a documentary, these frames are embedded into the fabric of the film itself and provide a guide to an audience for how to interpret its content. Some documentaries want the audience to forget about the presence of the camera, others want to draw their awareness to it, and still others vary the perspective based upon the narrative demands of the story at any given moment in time.

Observational Framing

One choice is to simply pretend that the camera is not there. This framing is as old as cinema itself. As MacDougall notes,

> When people began taking snapshots just before the turn of the [twentieth] century, they would say, "Look at the camera." Later, responding to a new impulse, they began to say, "Don't look at the camera. Go on with what you were doing." They wanted photographs of life, but as though photography had not occurred.
>
> Something similar happened in film. The directness of many of the "primitive" films made between 1895 and 1920 resulted from an acknowledgment of the act of filming. They were often about the specific historical moment when a cinematographer came to town. Later such scenes disappeared from the cinema, banished by a professionalism

that viewed any internal evidence of filmmaking as an aesthetic error. "As you know," Basil Wright once said, "as soon as someone looked at the camera, you threw that shot out because the illusion of reality had been lost."[6]

We should take a moment to marvel at that last statement. Wright acknowledges that the sense of documentary realism depended upon banishing all traces of actual realism from the finished product.

This impulse toward observational purity is very much alive in many verité documentaries today. It creates an experience that resembles the privileged, near-omniscient point of view of many fiction films. Characters interact exclusively with each other and the world around them, and through action they reveal the circumstances of their lives, just as in fiction films. When a documentary settles into observational mode, it presents a world that attempts to simulate what editor Aaron Wickenden refers to as "the illusion of unmediated experience." Its fundamental conceit is that *the camera was never there*, and it asks the viewers to become comfortable with an experience uncomplicated by the labor of its production.

The 2020 Academy Award nominee *Honeyland* was created in this observational vein and announces its intentions straight away. The first shot is of its beekeeper protagonist, Hatidze Muratova, crossing a very large field, shot from a high angle on a nearby cliff. The film then cuts to another angle that shows her walking directly toward the camera. There is no evident self-consciousness on her part as she walks purposefully to a nook in the rocks where she has one of her beehives. Later in the scene, she traverses a perilous passage on a cliff's edge that drops hundreds of feet just two or three feet to the left of her, yet she reveals no awareness or concern for the camera that is directly behind her (Figure 4.1).

Among other recent, well-known examples we would certainly include the 2021 Academy Award winner *My Octopus Teacher*, which shows protagonist Craig Foster taking video footage of his beloved octopus in the cold waters of the Atlantic Ocean on the south coast of South Africa but never acknowledges the camera shooting Foster

Figure 4.1 Hatidze Murtova walks near a cliff in *Honeyland*

himself. Some viewers intuitively feel the sleight of hand behind the "cinematic perfection" of this kind of filmmaking. For Richard Brody of *The New Yorker*, the elimination of the filmmakers' presence from *Honeyland* "makes an extraordinary true story feel fabricated" and became a major obstacle to his enjoyment of the film. "It's as if the reality of . . . the practical relationships of filmmaking were too messy and ambiguous for the filmmakers' tidy hermetic schema," he wrote.[7] David MacDougal had a related complaint about observational documentaries in general in 1998.

> By asking nothing of the subjects beyond permission to film them, the filmmaker adopts an inherently secretive position. There is no need for further explanation, no need to communicate with the subjects on the basis of the thinking that organizes the work. There is, in fact, some reason for the filmmaker not to do so for fear it may influence their behavior. In this insularity, the filmmaker withholds the very openness that is being asked of the subjects in order to film them.[8]

MacDougal suggests later in the passage that this practice of putting distance between observer and subject is a rather odd one when compared against the methods of inquiry used in other fields.

Scientific experiments are conducted by *actively intervening* in the world to test the outcome of a particular provocation. A journalist engages in an *active search* for information when reporting on a story. All other things being equal, this passive observational stance can be a rather evasive posture.

Yet in many cases the observational feel of a documentary is more of a cinematic construct than a lived reality, because a great deal of collaboration between filmmakers and participants often takes place behind the scenes. The glances at the camera and references to the act of filming, as well as other evidence of production (microphones, film lights, and cables in the shot) are all just removed in the editing room. In the production of *Honeyland*, for instance, directors Tamara Kotevska and Ljubomir Stefanov describe their interaction with Muratova as one of mutual respect, mutual benefit, and warm collaboration. In Muratova, they found a woman with a lifelong dream to have her beekeeping documented by a film crew, and a familial dynamic quickly developed.

> The first thing we would do when we got there in the morning to film was to have breakfast together. She always made really good coffee, and she always read our fortune in the coffee cup when we finished. She prepared food for us and we brought food for her, and would often cook on the fireplace in her yard.

This collaborative spirit extended to the filming as well. The previously mentioned opening sequence, in which Muratova is seemingly unaware of the camera, came about after days of patient research during which Muratova showed Kotevska and Stefanov all of the places she would walk. Muratova gladly obliged when the filmmakers asked her to embark on one of her walks so that they could shoot it. As filming went on, Muratova became more and more invested in the result and quietly came to see herself as having a stake in the completion of the film's storylines, one of which involved her elderly, ailing mother. Several scenes had already been shot of Muratova and her mother in the tiny bedroom of their ancient stone house with the two women seated in a nearly identical position each time, and when

Muratova's mother became acutely ill, Muratova intervened to facilitate the production. As co-director Tamara Kotevska described it,

> We were in the advanced editing phase, and Hatidze called us one day and told us, "She's dying." When we got there, there were relatives in the back. But Hatidze was keeping her mother in the same position for several hours. We think that's because she was aware that we needed to film that scene just as we had filmed the others.

This example shows the offscreen compact that is often created between filmmakers and participants about how the participants' onscreen role is to be performed with respect to their awareness of the camera, and how difficult it can be to impute the actual relationship between filmmaker and participant judging solely from the onscreen evidence. It can take extraordinary work to achieve the seemingly effortless flow of life caught unawares.

The Semi-staged Scene

Traces of filmmaker/participant collaboration are often hiding in plain sight in the form of what we might call the *semi-staged scene.* Here a documentary filmmaker may wish to reveal certain bits of emotional and narrative information to the audience but also wants to preserve the integrity of their observational presence framing (which would be broken by using an interview), so they come up with a compromise: invite the participant to engage in an interaction with another participant while the cameras are rolling. One of the set pieces of the 2019 music documentary *Echo in the Canyon* is an extended conversation among Jakob Dylan, Regina Spektor, Cat Power, and Beck, who sit in a well-appointed California living room with a stack of records from the Laurel Canyon folk scene conveniently placed on the coffee table before them.[9] As they muse about their love of the music, there is an undeniable sense that Dylan, who elsewhere in the film interviews icons from the era, is really doing an interview in a different form even though he frames no overt questions and does not direct the conversation. The gambit is somewhat obvious, because there is no other reason for these four to gather except to be together in the documentary.

A huge portion of the footage from the final five episodes of the French true crime saga *Soupçons* (known in the United States as *The Staircase*) has similar semi-staged scenes. Protagonist Michael Peterson talks at great length with his family members about the ongoing machinations of the murder case against him over the course of numerous verité dialogue scenes. In an eight-minute-long scene from Episode 12, for instance, the family sits around as they discuss the latest proceedings in the trial.[10] Just a few minutes later, he does a walk-and-talk with his two daughters as a moving camera converts the scene into a perfectly smooth tracking shot.[11] The family discussion surely would have occurred in a different form without intervention from the filmmaker, but the participants seem happy to play along.

Ditto with multiple scenes from *90 Day Fiancé*, a TLC reality show that follows couples seeking to marry with a K-1 visa. Couples will conveniently arrange themselves on park benches or around kitchen tables for heart-to-heart discussions with a camera present (Figure 4.2).[12]

Figure 4.2 A conversation between a couple in *90-Day Fiancé*

Figure 4.3 Daniela and Veasna in *Aging Out*

This conceit is not exclusive to reality shows. *Aging Out*, Roger Weisberg and Vanessa Roth's excellent film from 2004 about foster children aging out of the system into adulthood, contains multiple scenes between participants Daniela and Veasna discussing the challenges of raising their young child within the foster care system. Instead of following the pure verité ideal of hanging out for hours on end until a discussion naturally arises, the filmmakers nudge discussion in front of the camera in a gentle way (see Figure 4.3).[13] The intentions are much less sensationalistic than on reality television, but the methods are not dissimilar.

The Participatory Frame

With all the restrictions of the observational frame and all that must be left out of it in order to keep it pure, some filmmakers choose instead to bring aspects of the filmmaking project *inside* the frame of presence. The mildest version of this approach is the one taken by documentaries that utilize talking head interviews as part of their narrative strategy but refrain from putting the filmmaker onscreen. In this framing, the presence of the filmmaker is tacitly acknowledged by the fact that the participant is talking to someone offscreen, but the voice of the filmmaker asking the questions is excluded from the edit. Social issue documentaries often use this approach, using interview clips as a way of prosecuting the inquiry even as they are mixed with long stretches of otherwise uninterrupted observational verité material.

Not all interviews are created equal, however, and where participants direct their look has important implications for presence framing. Until the early 2010s, the dominant choice was to place the interviewer immediately to the side of the camera, resulting in a shot that shows the participant looking just slightly off-axis. More recently the direct-to-camera interview has become much more common. This creates a different dynamic in which the subject looks directly into the camera and is often used for films or shows that are meant to have a testimonial or confessional feeling to them. (It is a natural choice for *Intervention*, for instance, but would be an odd choice for most social issue documentaries.)

A more robust participatory frame is used in films that posit the filmmaker as an active character in the proceedings. *Minding the Gap* is a 2018 documentary directed by Bing Liu that announces its participatory intentions in the very first scene, as teenagers Bing (holding the camera), Zack, and Keire climb the fire escape of a tall building with their skateboards in tow.[14] Keire, ascending the stairs with evident trepidation, looks in the direction of the camera and says, "Bing, I think I'm gonna die." The film's setup, accomplished in a subsequent montage, makes the framing even more explicit. Bing yells "Take one!" and claps his hands together like a film slate. It's reinforced further when someone asks him, "Why are you filming everything?" and he responds off-camera, "Because I want to make a montage." This in turn is followed by two more quick shots in which the participants make overt mentions about Bing shooting them. All of this is in the service of establishing Bing as one of the main characters and teaching the audience about his role.

The fascinating thing about this section is that in order to fully introduce Bing by showing his face it is necessary to use a *second, unacknowledged camera*. In the shot in which Bing says, "Take one,"

Bing is the *subject*, with someone else doing the camera work (see Figure 4.4). The montage is so expertly edited that the average viewer pays no attention to this little cheat, but it technically violates the framing. (If Bing is the one with the camera, then who is filming *him*? The second camera person remains silent and is never introduced or acknowledged.) This is instructive, because it reinforces a larger point about framing: just because a film acknowledges the presence of the filmmaker, *it does not mean that it escapes framing as a construct.*

As the film continues, it makes deliberate choices to raise awareness of the act of filming in some scenes, when Bing is the focus of the story, and to diminish it in others, when the focus is shifted to Keire and Zack. For instance, Zack acknowledges the corporal punishment he received as a child, casually stating "When I was a kid and I was fucking up, I got my ass whooped; I think everyone does."[15] In this scene, the focus is on Zack, so Bing remains silent and there is no acknowledgment of his presence or of the act of filming. By contrast, the very next scene features Bing approaching his own house with a handheld camera and the rough production sound of the microphone jostling against the camera is *included* rather than eliminated. This instantly puts the focus of the shot on the fact that *Bing is filming*

Figure 4.4 The unacknowledged second camera shoots Bing Liu in *Minding the Gap*

this, which is helpful as an introduction to the next scene when he goes inside to reckon with the physical abuse that he suffered at the hands of his stepfather.

Narration and the Participatory Frame

Minding the Gap includes Bing as a central character in the film, but he does not use voice-over to narrate his story. The film thus plays out as the story of three boys, one of whom happens to be making the film, rather than as a proper first-person narrative. Anchoring a film with first-person narration changes the framing to place the author in a more overtly foregrounded position. There are many different flavors of this approach, each with its own particular logic. Alex Gibney often chooses to narrate his own films, framing the inquiry as an outgrowth of his personal curiosity. (In *Steve Jobs: The Man in the Machine* he narrates, "I wanted to know, was Jobs really so smart?" In *Citizen K* he says of Russian dissident Mikhail Khodorkovsky, "Khodorkovsky drew my interest at a time when we all seem haunted by Russia's role in the world, so I started a film about him.") Gibney's films often close with a monologue about the answers he has found on his journey, as he speaks of the ethics of the individual he has profiled and how their actions relate to the larger issues of the times. But Gibney almost never appears onscreen, preferring to narrate but remain largely absent from the film's visual universe.

Another approach allows the filmmaker to narrate as well as to play an active onscreen role. In Julie Shaw's *Living with Michael Jackson*, journalist Martin Bashir is heard chatting with Jackson about the documentary and negotiating with him over the terms of the filming; the developing relationship between the two men becomes part of the story. One of their first scenes, for instance, has Jackson expressing nervousness and shyness over showing Bashir various aspects of his life. ("Why do you do this to me?" Jackson complains sweetly about questions relating to his childhood.) As the film progresses, the relationship becomes more antagonistic, and Bashir's quest for a scoop becomes the unifying subtext of the film.

His persistent attempts to dig up new revelations about Jackson's activities, and the barriers put up by Jackson in opposition, are as much the subject of the film as are the creepy details about the pop star sleeping in the same bed with nine-year-old children. As the program draws to a close, an acknowledgment of the act of filming is explicitly employed to build anticipation for the final interview, in which the topics of Jackson's plastic surgery and the Neverland sleepovers will be discussed. "As we prepared for the interview,"[16] Bashir narrates dramatically, "the atmosphere was unusually tense." As the audience sees the film lights being put up around Jackson in preparation for said interview, Bashir continues: "There were unanswered questions, lots of them—areas of his life about which I felt he had been less than honest."

This approach of "filmmaker as intrepid crusader" is a minigenre of its own. Michael Moore has made a career out of playing the role of the conscientious, naive, mildly inept muckraker. Judith Helfand memorably turned a dispute with her parents over their choice to install vinyl siding on their house into a story about the dangers of toxic chemicals in *Blue Vinyl*. Ross McElwee played a version of himself in *Sherman's March*, which chronicled McElwee's comedic failures in his relationships with women. Each of these films presents the person onscreen as the author of the work who narrates a personal story in first-person singular. But Moore and Helfand do not operate their own camera, so the camera crew are the unacknowledged players placed outside of the frame of presence who make the documentation of the onscreen follies possible. McElwee *does* do his own shooting, and the results are mined for drama and laughs. In several scenes, the audience sees him navigate romantic relationships as he talks to girlfriends, and their reactions are made directly to the camera. In a memorable scene late in the film after several such pairings have gone awry, the film cuts to a female singer belting out Aretha Franklin's "Respect" in the parking lot of a strip mall, and the shot holds for an extra long time on her, zooming closer and closer. The audience can feel McElwee's longing simply by watching the camera roll, because the fusion of his authorial point of view and his literal point of view through the camera lens are so tightly fused.

Figure 4.5 Louis Theroux (right) interviews a former Scientology official in *My Scientology Movie*

The framing of presence in a documentary is not always consistent and can lead to disjointed messaging, as seen in Louis Theroux's *My Scientology Movie* (Figure 4.5). Theroux cut his teeth on Michael Moore's television show *TV Nation*, and one can feel Moore's influence on his style as he fashions himself as a bemused foreigner from the UK unearthing American oddities. The very title of the movie indicates an authorial role for Theroux, and he extends this impression by narrating in the first person just as Moore does. The audience sees him on camera directing the whole enterprise, from auditioning actors for the reenactments to jousting with Scientology officials who scream at him to get off their property, to conducting on-camera interviews with his subjects.

Yet the film's authorship is somewhat confused, as Theroux is also shown as an *interviewee* in numerous segments, talking to an unspecified interviewer just off camera (see Figure 4.6). "We've got actors coming in to play [Scientology leader] David Miscavige," he explains to this phantom filmmaker in the first of many such segments.

This filmmaker's voice is never heard, and the person's identity is mysterious right up until the end credits roll: "Directed by John Dower; Presented by Louis Theroux" (see Figures 4.7 and 4.8).

Figure 4.6 Louis Theroux is interviewed by an unnamed person in *My Scientology Movie*

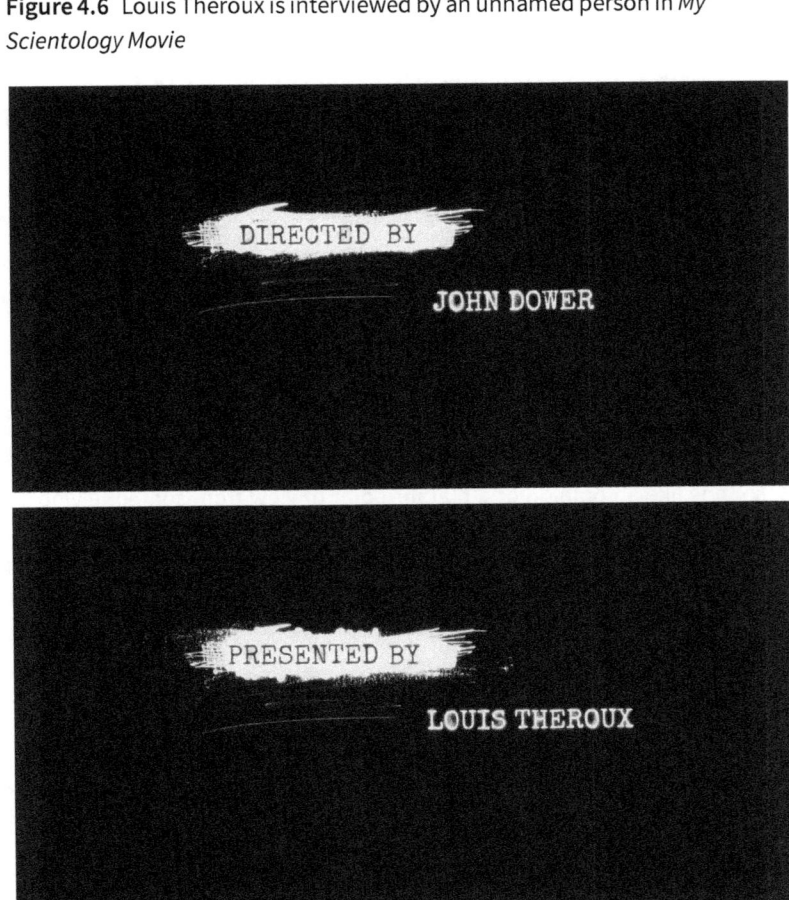

Figures 4.7 & 4.8 End credits in *My Scientology Movie*

It turns out that the "my" in the *My Scientology Movie* title refers to Dower, not Theroux.

Voice-of-God Narration

Not every narrator is attached to a particular persona. More traditional documentaries employ a "voice of God" narrator who speaks as the voice of the film but is not named and has no other presence. In essence, the traditional voice-over attempts to speak without much personalization at all, striving to achieve a neutral or "disinterested" tone. As one might imagine, managing a tone of neutrality while also providing emphasis and drama is a bit of a tightrope act. The narration must speak authoritatively, yet also avoid drawing too much attention to itself since its point is to embody a perspective that is theoretically objective and beyond opinion or feeling. Will Lyman, the voice of *Frontline* for over thirty-five years, spoke about precisely this calculation in an interview in 2008. Note how the issue of his presence is paramount.

In documentary narration, there's a certain line I try not to cross. It's hard to define that line, but I think of it as the point at which the viewer is listening to the wash of words and suddenly says, "Hang on a second, who's talking?" That will happen if the viewer hears what sounds like an opinion or a blatant point of view from someone who hasn't been properly introduced. If the narrator has also done an on-camera standup at the beginning of the show, or introduces himself personally as the "person who made this film," he or she can say whatever he likes. But, in the case of "Frontline," I am not introduced and therefore am not allowed by the viewer to give anything but information: no opinions, personal feelings, questioning of motives, et cetera. The trick, of course, is to come across, at the same time, as an involved and caring human being. After doing "Frontline" for 25 years now, I may have a little longer leash than I used to have and, in a recent program, actually referred to the filmmakers as "we." The producer and I were clearly betting that the audience had grown so accustomed to my voice that the use of the first person would be accepted, but it was a considered decision.[17]

In a series like this, all of whose episodes are produced by different production teams that may have no functional involvement with each other, Lyman's voice becomes the crucial unifying element and is a vital component of the Frontline brand. It is also notable that on the *Frontline* shows that are voiced by the individual producers/correspondents themselves, an intro segment will be cobbled together that positions Lyman as the *first* voice encountered by the viewer as he hands off the segment to the producer. ("Tonight, immigrant teenagers forced to work at farms that feed our families. . . . Reporter Daffodil Altan from the UC Berkeley Investigative Reporting Program goes inside a criminal conspiracy," he narrates at the top of the thirteenth episode from the thirty-sixth season of the show.)

Of course, "authoritative" and "disinterested" are not always the intended effect, and alternate tones of narration have a huge role in announcing a documentary's intentions—and the intended mode of reception. Brie Larson's role as narrator of *Fantastic Fungi* is both to convey factual information *and* to convey a sense of wonder and excitement for the biological processes of decomposition. Alternately, reverence for science is not the intended effect of the narration on the UK version of *Love Island*, a reality show that revels in its cheap thrills by way of a narrator who makes jokes about getting sloshed and wishing he could hook up with the contestants. Listening to the narration, the intended mode of consumption is clear: crack open a cold one with us and behold the parade of near-naked bodies.

Altering the Outcome

Seeming to go one step further toward transparency, some documentaries acknowledge not only the presence of the cameras and the filming process, but also the fact that the filmmakers have complicated relationships with the participants and that the filming affects the outcome of the events that it seeks to document. This was perhaps most famously accomplished in 1961 by anthropological filmmaker Jean Rouch and sociologist Edgar Morin in *The Chronicle of a Summer*, which marked the birth of so-called cinema verité filmmaking.[18] They saw their project as an experiment in ethnography, putting their own Parisian culture under the magnifying glass of the anthropological gaze. Morin waxed rhapsodic in comments made at the beginning of production, claiming that in their filming they would achieve a level of transparency never before attempted.

The first scene does not disappoint. Rouch and Morin sit in a small living room with one of their participants, Marceline (see Figure 4.9). The three openly discuss the barriers to an honest and unselfconscious conversation, with Rouch saying, "I don't know if we can succeed in recording as natural a conversation as we would without a camera present" and Marceline agreeing that it "won't be easy."[19] Nonetheless, they push ahead. Marceline gets involved with the project and becomes an interviewer herself as the growing collective of makers/subjects discuss the French-Algerian war, the presence of

Figure 4.9 Jean Rouch, Marceline Loridan-Ivans, and Edgar Morin in *The Chronicle of a Summer*

racism in modern France, the degradations of work, and the ennui of modern life. At the end, the audience witnesses a screening at which all of the participants discuss their reactions to seeing themselves onscreen.

Despite its patina of total transparency, this documentary, too, has a frame. Numerous encounters that read as spontaneous in the film were in fact set up by Rouch and Morin; many events are shown out of chronological order; and the film contains none of the contentious behind-the-scenes discussions that took place between the two directors about how to shape the film. Thus, the frame for *Chronicle of a Summer* is one that *simulates* a thoroughgoing honesty and reflexivity about the enterprise of filmmaking by ostentatiously including select scenes that gesture in that direction, even while taking other, hugely important events *out* of the frame. The truly revelatory document from this experiment is perhaps not the film itself, but the postfilm, postmortem essay. Concluding what he learned from the whole endeavor, Morin wrote,

> Finally we come to the problem of *cinema-verite*. How do we dare speak of a truth that has been chosen, edited, provoked, oriented, deformed? Where is the truth? At the end of the film, the difficulties of truth, which had not been a problem in the beginning, became apparent to me. In other words, I thought that we would start from a basis of truth and that an even greater truth would develop. Now I realize that if we achieved anything, it was to present the problem of the truth. We wanted to get away from comedy, from spectacles, to enter into direct contact with life. But life itself is also a comedy, a spectacle. Better (or worse) yet: each person can only express himself through a mask, and the mask, as in Greek tragedy, both disguises and reveals, becomes the speaker. In the course of the dialogues, each one was able to be more real than in daily life, but at the same time more false.[20]

The Reflexive Frame

Is it possible to escape the framing of presence and arrive at fully transparent relationship between filmmaker, camera, and subject?

As one might imagine, doing this involves attacking the basis on which meaning is made in the first place. One of the most thoughtful practitioners of such an approach is Trinh T. Minh-ha, a filmmaker who has also written extensively about the process of making meaning in documentary film.

Her 1982 film *Reassemblage*, shot in Senegal, accomplishes this goal by rejecting nearly every documentary filmmaking convention in the book (Figure 4.10). Sound and picture are often mismatched and out of sync. Cuts are made in seemingly arbitrary ways and without respect for any of the conventions of continuity editing. Even the narration pushes back against the usual privileges of authorship. "I am not going to speak about, but [rather] speak nearby," she says in a whisper, rejecting the easy confirmatory relationship between words and pictures we discussed in Chapter 2. Whenever the audience starts to get comfortable and momentarily disappears into the illusion of the film as an uncomplicated window

Figure 4.10 Trinh T. Minh-Ha's *Reassemblage*

onto the pro-filmic reality that it depicts, a radical jump cut or jarring picture/sound mismatch will occur to jolt them back to the actual circumstances: the audience is sitting in a room somewhere, watching a movie. Instead of the uncomplicated meanings and strong emotions prized by most filmmakers, Minh-ha is in search of "a documentary aware of its own artifice."[21]

Minh-ha's thoughts on documentary shooting are also instructive. Instead of approaching her work with professionalism (creating clean, smooth panning shots, for instance), she likes shots that contain reminders of the labors of production.

> I usually shoot with no fore practice and often with only one eye. . . . I may at times shoot the same subject more than once, but . . . the first time always turns out to be the best, because when one repeats the gesture one becomes sure of oneself. What I value is the hesitation or whatever happens when I first encounter what I am seeing through the camera lens.

These imperfections are celebrated precisely because they refuse to divorce the product (the shot) from the process (the shooting.) All in all, Minh-ha's goal is to communicate on a level that *rejects* the trance of the standard cinema experience and does not facilitate an easy creation of meaning in the audience's imagination.

It may come as no surprise to note that this is not a commercially lucrative mode of filmmaking. Its motivations are deconstructionist in nature, and it does not accede to any of the common expectations that audiences carry when they apprehend a new film or show. Precisely because of that, it is also interesting to ponder whether such a film is effective at communicating its intended meaning without the benefit of an extrafilmic explanation such as those provided in her writings. Do most audiences, conditioned to decode framing cues but not the underpinnings of the framing impulse itself, come to any of her desired conclusions by watching the film on its own, or do they simply see a confusing piece of noncinema made by an academic? This is the gamble taken by any filmmaker daring to challenge heavily ingrained ideas of what film structure is and should be, and points up the need to think critically about the expectations audiences carry into any viewing experience. To decode a film, perhaps a frame is *always* necessary, and in the case of *Reassemblage*, it takes the form of her essay "The Totalizing Quest for Meaning."

Notes

1. David MacDougall, *Transcultural Cinema* (Princeton, NJ: Princeton University Press, 1998), 201.
2. This concept has similarities to, but is not coterminous with, Bill Nichols's schema of documentary modes. Each of Nichols's modes includes a broad range of attributes, presumptions, and concerns that characterize it. (The rhetorical element is underdeveloped in the poetic mode, for instance, and the participatory mode necessarily involves the ethics and politics of the encounter between filmmaker and subject.) "Presence framing," by contrast, is a term specifically concerned with the putative relationship between the filmmaker, the camera, and the participants.
3. As Bill Nichols says, "All discourses, including documentary film, seek to externalize evidence—to place it referentially outside the domain of the discourse itself." Bill Nichols, *Speaking Truths with Film* (Oakland: University of California Press, 2016), 99.
4. Veerle Ros, Jennifer M. J. O'Connell, Miklos Kiss, and Annelies van Noortwijk, "Toward a Cognitive Definition of First-Person Documentary," in *Cognitive Theory and Documentary Film*, ed. Caitlin Brylla and Mettte Kramer (Cham: Palgrave Macmillan, 2018), 229.
5. Marvin Minsky, "A Framework for Representing Knowledge," in *Readings in Cognitive Science*, ed. Allan Collins and Edward E. Smith (Morgan Kauffman, 1988), 158.
6. MacDougall, *Transcultural Cinema*, 202.
7. Richard Brody, ""Honeyland" Reviewed: A Gripping, Frustrating Documentary about A Beekeeper's Fragile Isolation," *The New Yorker*, August 1, 2019. https://www.newyorker.com/culture/the-front-row/honeyland-reviewed-a-gripping-frustrating-documentary-about-a-beekeepers-fragile-isolation.
8. MacDougall, *Transcultural Cinema*, 202.
9. *Echo in the Canyon*, directed by Andrew Slater (Greenwich Entertainment, 2018), 00:08:02.
10. *The Staircase*, directed by Jean-Xavier de Lestrade (Maha Productions, 2018), 00:15:00–00:22:50.

11. As the show cuts from a wide shot behind the three subjects to this tracking shot, careful observers will note that they have moved from a bucolic wooded area to a leafy parking lot. *The Staircase*, 00:26:30.

12. The scene shown in Figure 4.2 is taken from Episode 5, Season 4 of *90 Day Fiancé* (Sharp Entertainment, 2019).

13. *Aging Out*, directed by Roger Weisberg, Maria Finitzo, and Vanessa Roth (Public Policy Productions, 2004), 00:18:45.

14. A fourth character, Kyle, is also present. His role is minimized in the film, however, to keep the focus on these three main protagonists.

15. *Minding the Gap*, directed by Bing Liu (ITVS / Kartemquin Films, 2018), 00:32:10.

16. *Living with Michael Jackson*, directed by Julie Shaw (Granada Television, 2003), 01:17:00 .

17. "The Soup Cans Interview: Will Lyman," *Soup Cans*, October 7, 2008, http://soupcans.blogspot.com/2008/10/soup-cans-interview-will-lyman.html.

18. It is important to note the difference that once existed in terminology between "cinema verité" and "observational cinema" (or "direct cinema"). For a period of time in the 1960s and 1970s, verité was associated with the highly participatory approach of Rouch, while observational referred to the seemingly hands-off method represented by filmmakers like Frederick Wiseman. As time has passed, the term "verité" has become a catch-all phrase that refers to any documentary material of spontaneous moments happening in front of a camera, usually handheld.

19. *The Chronicle of a Summer*, directed by Jean Rouch and Edgar Morin (Argos Films, 1961), 00:03:43.

20. Edgar Morin, "Chronicle of a Film," in *The Documentary Film Reader: History, Theory, Criticism*, ed. Jonathan Kahan (Oxford: Oxford University Press, 2016), 471.

21. Trinh T. Minh-ha, "The Totalizing Quest for Meaning," in *Theorizing Documentary*, ed. Michael Renov (New York: Routledge, 1993), 99.

5

Flow

As we noted at the start of Chapter 1, documentaries are collages. One discontinuous slice of experience follows another in a hodgepodge of interview bites, archival clips, verité moments, reenactments, and onscreen titles and graphics. Yet to produce the desired effect—a coherent experience of wonder, drama, and surprise—the filmmaker somehow has to sheer off the hard edges of the individual clips. Their documentary needs *flow*.

Flow is the way that you are led from one idea to the next without interruption or distraction; it is the river that your little boat of consciousness is floating upon; it is the very fact that you do not notice the cuts. In a conventional documentary, this progression of ideas will feel both effortless and as solid as steel.

Unifying with Sound

The buffing of hard edges starts at the level of the individual cut. When two shots are placed next to one another as raw clips, viewers are presented with both a visual break (the cut) *and* a break in audio as they hear a harsh change in the background sounds that accompany the picture. Cuts like these feel "hard," as viewers are presented with an unmistakable break in continuity. Even if the progression of ideas from one clip to the next is logical and seamless, it can be hard for audiences to latch onto because of this very distracting auditory break.

Filmmakers long ago seized on a basic fact of our evolutionary instincts—abrupt noises trigger our response mechanisms, but

How Documentaries Work. Jacob Bricca, Oxford University Press. © Oxford University Press 2023.
DOI: 10.1093/oso/9780197554104.003.0006

continuous sound goes unnoticed—and used it to smooth over these interruptions. When a continuous background sound is added to a series of discontinuous clips, it bridges the visual breaks in a "unifying sound bath," as Michel Chion puts it, resulting in a sequence that feels continuous.[1] Two clips that before seemed to have nothing to do with one another suddenly seem perfectly natural side by side. This can take the form of added ambient noises (birdsong, traffic), music, or simply a consistent level of background noise (see Figure 5.1).

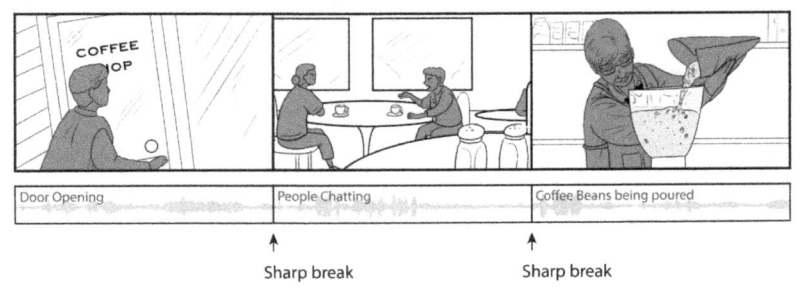

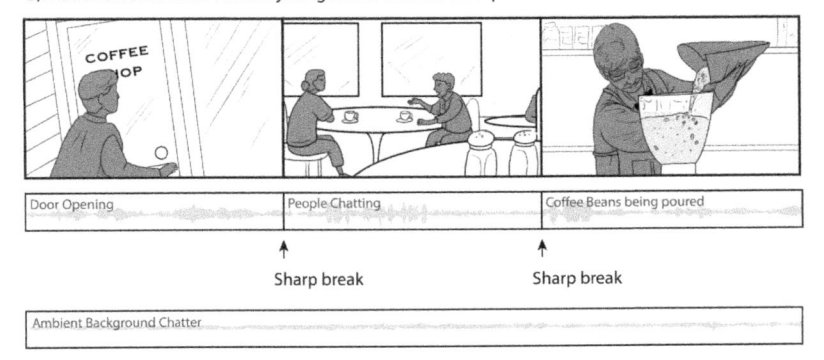

Figure 5.1 Continuous background sound unifies disparate shots
Illustration by Kaylah Rasmussen.

This practice alone does not create flow, however. Enter the *pre-lap*. The pre-lap (also known as the "J-Cut") is a simple but powerful tool that introduces the audio from a new clip a moment *before* the picture cut occurs. As the film is chugging along, a new sound—the beginning of a new sentence of dialogue, or the background sound of a new verité clip—effortlessly arrives (see Figure 5.2). Subconsciously viewers wonder, *"What's that?"* and before they know it the picture associated with the sound appears.

Without pre-laps, documentary subjects begin talking only once they are seen and the audience must wait until the end of their sentence before seeing something new, creating a herky-jerky experience that never becomes more than the sum of its parts. With the pre-lap, the cut feels satisfying rather than frustrating, inevitable rather than arbitrary, as the audience is pulled into the upcoming clip by the sound, which is then redeemed by the picture. It's over before viewers even notice what's going on, but, as with the micronarratives discussed in Chapter 3, they have instantly had the satisfaction of a question silently asked and answered.

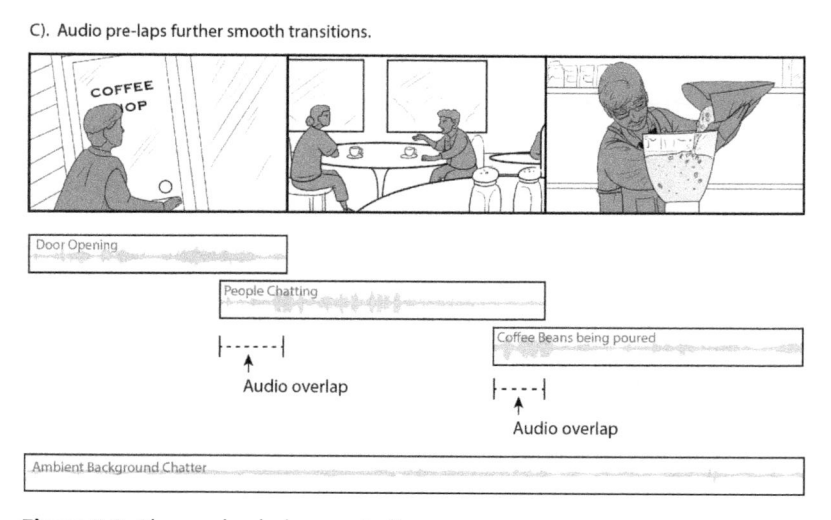

C). Audio pre-laps further smooth transitions.

Figure 5.2 The pre-lap helps create flow
Illustration by Kaylah Rasmussen.

Pivots and Pauses

With the preceding techniques, a documentary can string together a series of clips into a coherent scene. But what happens when a documentary needs to shift from one scene to the next? How is this kind of flow achieved?

At the thirty-minute mark of the 2019 documentary *Diego Maradona*, we find an answer. The man named by the international soccer magazine *Four Four Two* as "the greatest footballer ever" is at the very height of his fame.[2] Murals of him are going up both in his hometown of Buenos Aires, Argentina, and in his adopted home of Naples, Italy, where he plays for Napoli. Fellow soccer player Gennaro Montuori recalls that "almost every Neapolitan had a photo of Diego in their homes . . . many had it on top of their bed, next to Jesus."

The audience then hears the click of a 35 mm camera as a photo from the era shows Maradona posing with a small group of adoring fans. The camera clicks again, and he is seen in a different location posing with a different fan. A third click is heard and a third photo appears, this time with several women with their arms draped over him. Four more snaps are heard, each paired with a different photo of him surrounded by fans of all ages. Then a final snap is heard, and a final picture takes the screen: Maradona smiles broadly beside a curly-haired man in a red suit with a cocktail in his hand. The two are close; they seem to be best friends. As the image lingers, the camera zooms in slowly on the man next to him as foreboding music can be heard faintly and the audience realizes that the man is Carmine Giuliano, who was introduced earlier in the film as the head of the Camorra crime family. Now the film cuts to a video clip of the same man, and as he begins to speak a lower-third title card identifies him as "Carmine Giuliano" with an ominous title below him reading: "Camorra Boss."

What you've just witnessed is a quintessential example of a documentary *pivot*, which is another crucial but nearly invisible element of flow. Whether called handoffs, turns, or pivots, the idea is the same.[3] The film was following one idea—*Maradona is adored by*

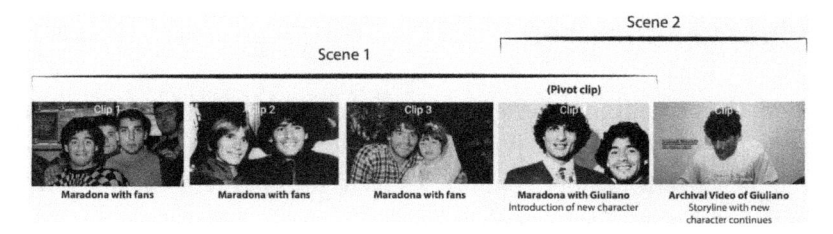

Figure 5.3 The pivot clip delicately redirects audience attention
Illustration by Kaylah Rasmussen.

fans, and everyone wants a piece of him—then pivoted to the next idea—*Maradona seems to have become friendly with the Camorra mob family, who also want a piece of him.*[4] The crucial shot here was the one of the two men together, which is the only clip that belongs to both scenes (see Figure 5.3).

The eight-second-long pivot clip takes the first idea and steers it toward a new one. As the audience watches the film, they at first think this is just one more of Maradona's fans, but the pause and the zoom trigger the next scene. By contrast, a documentary with a less evolved sense of flow might cut to black after the fan photos and then start with a new interview clip discussing the Camorra crime family as if the two were wholly separate ideas.

For another example, let's look to the outstanding documentary series *America to Me*, which follows the lives of a number of students at Oak Park and River Forest High School (OPRF) in suburban Chicago. This public high school prides itself on its racial diversity and high test scores, but it is also a site of great racial tension, and the series is a nuanced and insightful interrogation of how race plays into nearly every aspect of these students' lives. Early in the first episode, we meet Ke'Shawn Kumsa, a smart and sociable junior who tells us by way of introduction, "Most people say I have a great personality, [but] they [also] say sometimes I goof off. . . . That's pretty accurate!" Ke'Shawn owns his flaws but also goes on to point out how he dislikes being judged by teachers because of the color of his skin.

Ke'Shawn is then called to the front of the room by his chemistry teacher to fix something in his notebook. Ke'Shawn is unhappy being singled out in this way, and he responds to his teacher with forced, sarcastic civility. As if to underscore his dislike of the situation, he says in an interview, "There's nothing at OPRF that I can't get at another school. I just feel, what's the big deal about Oak Park?" Looking now right at the interviewer, he becomes very direct: "I'm actually asking *you* that question; I really don't know. I don't know what the big deal is, actually." The film then takes a longer-than-average pause as Ke'Shawn looks perplexed.

Cut to an aerial drone shot of the school. A music cue full of intrigue commences, and the narrator takes up the thread. "The big deal about Oak Park is a pride in its history: home to Ernest Hemingway and Frank Lloyd Wright . . . Renowned chemist Percy Julian was the first African American to move here in the 1950s, though his home was firebombed twice." The film is now sailing through a brief history of OPRF as an important living example of racial integration as well as continuing racial strife. In this case, the closing comments of Ke'Shawn ("What's the big deal?") was the pivot point to the "history of OPRF" scene. The end of one clip has matched up in a fortuitous way with the beginning of the next one, thanks to some clever narration ("The big deal about Oak Park is . . .").

Most documentaries have dozens of pivots over the course of their running time. These pivots exist to subtly steer the storytelling direction of a film, allowing it to push forward in its narrative and deepen its drama. Part of the pleasure of a well-constructed documentary is the dexterity with which the film shapes flow. Scene 1, *pivot*, Scene 2, *pivot*, Scene 3, *pivot* . . . And so on.

It's useful to note that when making a change of topic, a film will almost always place a subtle pause in the pivot clip. In the case of *Diego Maradona*, the last photo is held onscreen for over twice the length of any of the previous photos, creating a sense of suspended animation as the film subtly zooms in on the shady character next to Maradona. In the case of the *America to Me* clip, the pause is on the tail end of the interview clip with Ke'Shawn, which holds for a pregnant pause after he says, "I don't know what the big deal is, actually." These pauses are subtle, but they are crucial.

What exact function do the pauses serve? To answer this question, think for a moment about the importance of paragraphs in the written word. Stories of all kinds (fiction, journalism, etc.) are rarely told in one long, breathless excretion, but rather in chunks, with *paragraphs*. To initiate a new paragraph requires no words, but when the reader encounters a new paragraph, an invisible signal is sent: *there is something different between the section that just concluded and the one that's about to come. Expect a pivot.* When paragraphs are not used, perfectly good writing becomes awkward and difficult to follow; it feels disorganized as it veers from one topic to the next without a break. The pause is the documentary's version of a paragraph break. By spending just a little bit longer waiting on the silence after a certain quotation or visual moment, it makes the next cut feel like something novel, creating both emphasis and separation. It lets the import of one thought sink in before the next one is introduced.

Juxtaposition

In all the preceding examples, the film directs an audience's attention from topic to topic with gentle, delicate maneuvering. But what happens when the flow of meaning is purposefully broken and a blunter juxtaposition is offered? Now a different kind of experience is achieved because the meanings created become more *implicit* and *subtextual.* Instead of laying out the connection between the scenes in an explicit way, the clips are simply placed alongside each other, and the audience is challenged to find the meaning themselves, with the *separation* between the ideas becoming the source of the film's dramatic power.

For an example, take the 1997 Errol Morris film *Fast, Cheap & Out of Control*, which profiles the work of a lion tamer, a robotics engineer, a topiary artist, and an expert on naked mole rats. The film begins with a visually rich but fundamentally mysterious scene featuring imagery of lions, robots, hairless rodents, and oddly shaped shrubs. The placement of the clips together in one single montage silently expresses the key conceit of the film: *there must be a connection between these worlds.* (The title also does some heavy lifting here—it promises cheap thrills even though the content of the film is actually rather cerebral.)[5] The film then proceeds for the next eighty minutes to give the audience dozens of thirty- to ninety-second segments from each of the four protagonists. Within each segment the storytelling is straightforward, with interview-as-narration providing clear guidance and delivering discrete stories and statements. But from segment to segment, the audience is left to their own devices. No pivots are offered, only the silent provocation created by the absence of connecting tissue.

The 2012 Danish/Polish co-production *Polish Illusions* provides another example. The film oscillates between two storylines in an unnamed Pomeranian town in northwest Poland. In one, an elderly magician fruitlessly searches for his next performance opportunity as he waxes nostalgic about the full employment of the Communist era (Figure 5.4). In the other, a brash, retired American expat helicopter pilot searches for love and is followed around by a young Polish acolyte who adores his seemingly unflappable bravado and his vast range of military vehicles (Figure 5.5). Each of the two stories offers a conventional problem/solution structure—Will the

Figure 5.4 A Polish magician in *Polish Illusions*

Figure 5.5 An American expat in *Polish Illusions*

magician eventually get a gig? Will the expat pilot find a mate?—but there is no overlap or intersection between the stories. The juxtaposition between the two creates a productive friction and opens up an empty space that must be filled by the audience. *What is meant by placing these two disconnected stories side by side?* The inability of the magician to adapt to the post-Communist, free-market environment, and the fascination of the young Pole with the American, coupled with the film's title, hints toward a critical commentary on Polish national identity. "Yes, it is a provocative title," said co-director Jacob Dammas, who stuck with the title even after a third character, a Danish man who tried in vain to become a small-time real estate developer along the Polish coast, dropped out of the film. "We wanted to show this universal struggle to be recognized for your worth, which all the characters are searching for as the shadow of history looms large over them. We also wanted to leave it as open as possible for the audience to get something out of the film for themselves."

Any documentary operating on this level of abstraction tends to have some other method of generating coherence to keep the program from generating undue confusion or impatience. These methods can be thematic, formal, or narrative in nature.

In *Fast, Cheap & Out of Control*, they are primarily thematic. The connections between the stories at first seem to be superficial. The lion tamer and the naked mole rat researcher work directly with animals; the topiary artist creates living sculptures in the shapes of animals; the robotics engineer programs his creatures to maneuver their legs like insects. As the film goes on, the connections get deeper. Though none of the men ever uses the phrase "trial and error," they all talk about the iterative processes they use in their work. As the film progresses even further, the connections become even more profound as each man wrestles with fundamental questions of consciousness. The rodent expert and the lion tamer each wonder aloud about how much awareness the animals have about their own existence. The robotics engineer posits that with rapid advances in technology, self-awareness may soon be the only functional difference between humans and robots. By the end, the scope of the film cues its audience to ask such deep philosophical questions as "What is the nature of consciousness?" and "How much of the behavior of any animal, including humans, is motivated by instinct versus free will?" The remarkable thing about the film is that none of the protagonists ever brings these questions up themselves; the meaning is created purely through inference and juxtaposition.

Thematic threads are also woven through documentary cinematographer Kirsten Johnson's *Cameraperson*, which plays out as a succession of fifty-three discrete scenes culled from twenty-four different films that she shot over the course of her twenty-year career. A young boxer heads out into the ring in Brooklyn, New York; a baby is born in the maternity ward of a hospital in Kano, Nigeria; a cityscape shot of Sarajevo, Bosnia, is seen as Johnson talks off-camera to the director about how to frame the shot. As in *Fast, Cheap & Out of Control*, there at first seems to be little connection between the individual scenes, but certain themes slowly start to emerge: war, human trauma, the act of remembrance, the meaning of motherhood. Crucially in this film, there are also formal connections between scenes that provide adhesive material. Scene 14 is a close-up shot of a teenage girl's hands as she explains her feeling of guilt for having allowed herself to become pregnant ("I feel like a bad female"); three scenes later, a nearly

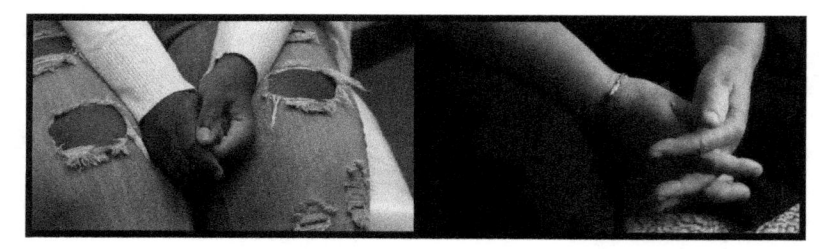

Figure 5.6 Two Scenes from *Cameraperson*

identical shot features the hands of a former resident of Sarajevo as she gives quiet, understated testimony about torture and rape that took place during the period of ethnic cleansing (see Figure 5.6). Scene 15 ends with a shot of the green grasslands of Wyoming, and Scene 16 begins with a shot of grasslands in Foča, Bosnia. There are also subtle narrative threads that punctuate the film at intervals. The boxer who went out into the ring in Scene 3 is seen again near the end of the film in Scene 50 as he angrily enters his locker room following the fight, then returns to the arena to find his mother in the stands, who hugs him tightly. The scenes of Johnson interacting amiably with *her* mother, who is frequently confused by the events unfolding around her because of her advanced Alzheimer's, give way to scenes that feature Johnson's twins playing in the background with their grandfather as the camera shows the urn containing her mother's ashes. And in the longest running narrative thread of the film, eight of the film's fifty-three scenes are vignettes from Bosnia involving material related to the war and atrocities committed there, including a trio of scenes with one particular family. As with the other films mentioned here, it is the superficial disconnection between rest of the scenes that, when coupled with these small formal and narrative threads, leads to a feeling of powerful universality.

It's also interesting to point out that *Cameraperson* utilized a much more conventional structure in its rough-cut incarnations before the final cut was reached. The first draft of the film took over a year of editing to complete and put Johnson in the role of narrator, commenting throughout on her experiences shooting survivors of rape, torture, and war. "When the lights came up on that cut," said producer Marilyn Ness, "the first thing I said to Kirsten was, 'Please tell me you have a therapist.' . . . It was a lot of genocides, a lot of rape, a lot of very sick babies being born." Ness was convinced that 120 minutes of uninterrupted misery and unprocessed trauma was going to be too much for any audience.[6]

Going back to the drawing board, Johnson and her team also realized that the narration was too omnipresent. It may have accurately reflected her own preoccupations, but it did not contain enough perspective to make the experience cathartic or redeeming for an audience; it was also not interesting to hear her state her thoughts so explicitly and to lead the audience in such a didactic way. She handed the footage over to editor Nels Bangerter, who built an entirely new version without voice-over. This was a revelation to all involved, including Johnson, who found that she was still very much present in the film even though her narration was now gone. In the film, Johnson can sometimes be heard from behind the camera talking to the subjects or to herself, and the activation of her presence is particularly strong in the opening scenes, which include a single title card written in the first person (see Figure 5.7). What results is a transmission of many of the sentiments heard in the original voice-over narration, but via subtext instead of text.

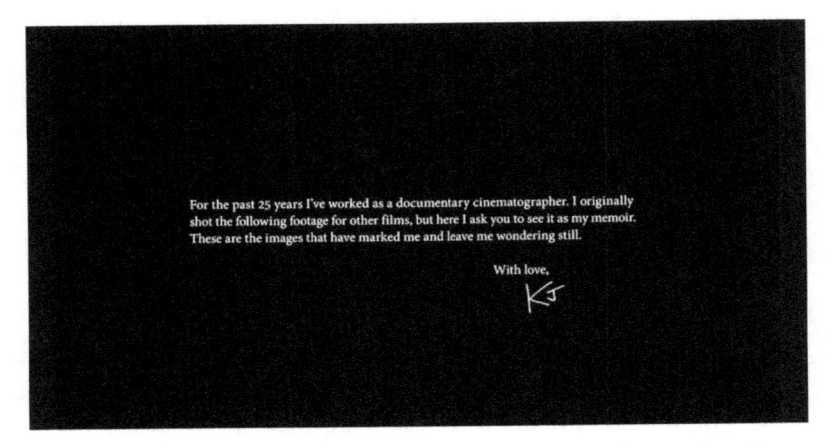

Figure 5.7 Kirsten Johnson's message to the audience at the opening of *Cameraperson*

Collective Memory

It's important to note that documentaries like this which rely on inference and juxtaposition also often rely on the assumed common knowledge and collective memory of their audience to create their meaning. Since the audience is called upon to "fill in the blanks," they must refer to memories and experiences beyond the boundaries of the film. *Polish Illusions* plays very differently to an American, who may pick up on the themes of capitalism versus communism, than it does to a Pole or a German, whose experiences in World War II make it a film whose themes of nationalism and identity play much stronger.

It is also sobering to look back on a film like Emile deAntonio's *Millhouse* in this regard. *Millhouse* was considered a savage indictment of Richard Nixon when it was released in 1971, with critics calling it "devastating" and saying that it "revealed the true horror of Nixon's personality."[7] Watching it today, one could be forgiven for wondering what all the fuss was about. With the details of the Watergate scandal now a distant memory and the outrageous antics of the Trump presidency fresh in the public's consciousness, the film comes across as bland and frequently confusing. There are implied references to numerous tidbits of history from the era that would have been common knowledge to an audience of the time, but, without viewers holding that history fresh in their minds, these bits no longer create the same meaning.

Godfrey Reggio's masterful *Koyaanisqatsi* suffers a similar fate. The 1983 film features images of nature in juxtaposition with fast-moving shots of traffic, cityscapes, and large housing developments meant to evoke the anonymity and inhumanity of modern life, along with numerous shots of weapons tests meant to convey the horror of a potential nuclear holocaust. Yet the critique of technology plays very differently now that many of the same stop-motion techniques (and even a few of the actual shots) have been co-opted by advertising, and the numerous shots of gigantic explosions generally fail to horrify now that climate change has eclipsed nuclear war as the existential threat of our times. The film also carries a subtle critique of television with its sequence showing a mother and children seemingly glued to the screen in a mall; but with old-fashioned network television now looked upon nostalgically as a heartwarming ritual of collective cultural bonding (as opposed to today's fragmented audiences and diminished attention spans), the reference goes dead. If the responses from my students at the University of Arizona are any indication, the film is still a thoroughly cinematic experience and remains thought-provoking to contemporary audiences, but in a way that is fundamentally different from someone watching it in the 1980s. The meaning in any documentary is always dependent upon the audience's collective memory in order to complete the circle of meaning.

Notes

1. Michel Chion, *Audio-Vision: Sound on Screen*, 2nd ed. (New York: Columbia University Press, 2019), 37.
2. Paul Sarahs, "The 50 Greatest Footballers of All Time," *FourFourTwo*, January 7, 2021, https://www.fourfourtwo.com/us/gallery/50-greatest-footballers-all-time.
3. Editor Michael Harte calls them "handoffs." Editor Aaron Wickenden, ACE calls them "turns."
4. The connection between Maradona and the Camorra crime family was seeded earlier in the film when it showed the head coach of the Naples team respond angrily to a press conference question about the influence of the Camorra crime family as Maradona looked on.
5. The title is taken from the title of a journal article coauthored by Rodney Brooks, the robot scientist in the film. Rodney A. Brooks and Anita M. Flynn, "Fast, Cheap and Out of Control: A Robot Invasion of the Solar System," *Journal of the British Interplanetary Society* 42, no. 10 (1989): 478.
6. From the short film *Editing "Cameraperson": Twenty-Five Years in the Making*, included as an extra on the Criterion Collection Blu-ray and DVD release of the film.
7. "Millhouse, a White Comedy," *Time Out*, https://www.timeout.com/en_gb/film/millhouse-a-white-comedy.

6

Time

Documentaries are inextricably bound to their status as a time-based art form. Unlike books, which can be read at any pace the reader chooses, or photography, which also leaves the duration of the encounter up to the viewer, documentaries fully control the viewer's experience of time. This of course involves pacing, but it also involves a more fundamental conceit. From the first frame to the last, these films seek to convince the audience that what they see onscreen *actually happened.*

Now, you may be saying to yourself, *Of course it happened; that's what makes it a documentary*, and in so saying you would be partially correct. Each individual shot *is* a recording of an encounter that actually took place. Yet the amalgam of shots arranged together in a documentary represent an experience that has no other referent in the real world. As we will see, this fundamental fact is crucial to remember as we think about how audience members experience the passage of time in a documentary.

The Experience of Time in Verité

When a documentary film or television show is presenting verité scenes, it imparts the illusion that what took place onscreen is what the audience would have seen if they were standing in the room at the time of filming. The conceit at play is that a cut simply represents a shift in point of view on the scene, as if there were multiple cameras running and someone just shifted from one camera to another like in the broadcast of a live sporting event.[1] But since verité scenes are usually shot with a single camera, this is rarely the case.

How Documentaries Work. Jacob Bricca, Oxford University Press. © Oxford University Press 2023.
DOI: 10.1093/oso/9780197554104.003.0007

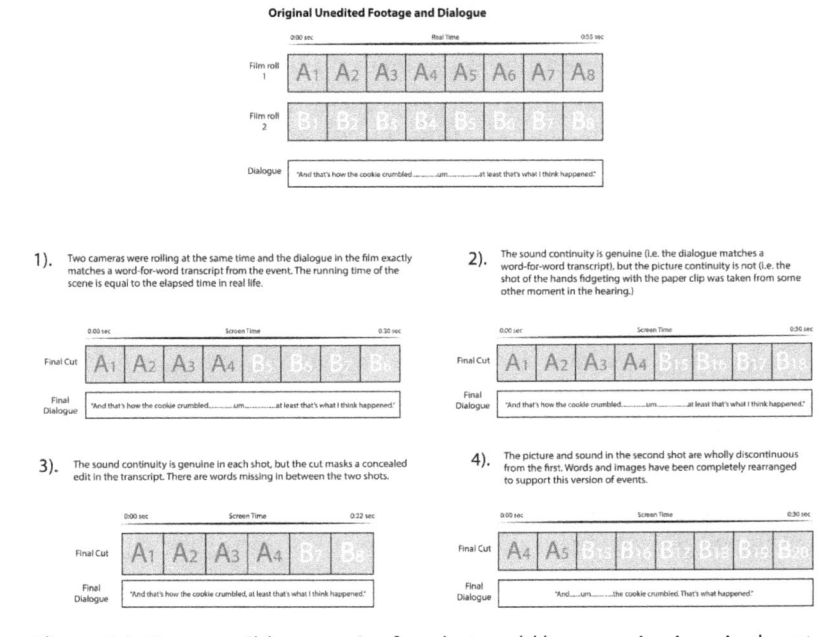

Figure 6.1 Four possible scenarios for what could be occurring in a single cut in a verité scene

Illustration by Kaylah Rasmussen.

Let's consider a hypothetical scene: in a hearing at the National Assembly in Ecuador, a senior public official faces accusations of misconduct. As she prepares to respond, the film cuts to her hands playing nervously with a paper clip, the voice of her interrogator continuing offscreen. As seen in Figure 6.1, any one of following things could be occurring in this single cut.

1. Two cameras were rolling at the same time and the dialogue in the film exactly matches a word-for-word transcript from the event. The running time of the scene is equal to the elapsed time in real life.
2. The sound continuity is genuine (i.e., the dialogue matches a word-for-word transcript), but the picture continuity is not

(i.e., the shot of the hands fidgeting with the paper clip was taken from some other moment in the hearing.)

3. The sound continuity is genuine within each shot, but the cut masks a concealed edit in the transcript. There are words missing in between the two shots.

4. The picture and sound in the second shot are wholly discontinuous from the first. Words and images have been completely rearranged to support this version of events.[2]

In everyday documentary practice, the fourth option is the most common. Even when two or more cameras are used to shoot a scene, the purpose of having them is not to faithfully reproduce the original conversation but to provide more opportunities for rearranging it. This is made possible by breaking the scene up into various overlapping visual fields of information. (The wide shot shows everything in the scene, whereas medium shots and close-ups show a subset of the whole.)

Add to this basic illusion a supplementary one, which is the pace at which events seem to take place. A verité scene may be edited to feel placid or fretful, languid or quick. The feeling of time is embedded into the fabric of the experience and seems to emanate from the reality of the situation rather than from the work of the film.

We can also identify a close variant of pure verité, which we'll call *accelerated verité*. In this mode, the attempt to simulate real time is abandoned in favor of an experience that is acknowledged to be faster than real life but not entirely divorced from it. Whereas a full-on montage often throws together images from a variety of times and places, this mode hangs onto verité as its stylistic touchstone even as it sometimes acknowledges discontinuity via the use of jump cuts.

Gaga: Five Foot Two, the authorized documentary profile of Lady Gaga, engages in this kind of relationship to time. The film conveys the pressure of sky-high expectations from fans, a relentless recording and touring schedule, and Gaga's own perfectionist tendencies. It does this in part by modulating the audience's experience of time. Most of the scenes in the first two-fifths of the film are played in pure verité with frequent but clearly distinguished montages often sandwiched between them; but as the film's pace quickens in order to convey the increasing pressures of her life, more and more of the verité scenes are punctuated with jump cuts that push the audience more aggressively forward in time, and the pacing in general accelerates.

Stray, Elizabeth Lo's film about the life of stray dogs in Istanbul, features several sections that take place in this mode. In an introductory sequence near the beginning of the film, the camera follows Zeytin, a beautiful light brown dog with expressive eyes and a calm manner, as she patiently roams the streets. There is a clear logic to the progression of scenes—she navigates the crossing of a busy street and then heads to calmer locales, for instance—but each scene tends to interrupt the one before by keeping Zeytin in the frame rather than gesturing to conventions of continuity by having her exit the frame before the next moment begins.[3]

The Interleaving of Scenes

Another way that documentaries push their stories forward through time is to complicate the usual separation between scenes. Traditionally one scene must end before another begins, but what happens when the filmmaker starts to chip away at the lines of separation between them? A look at a sequence from the opening of the Joe Berlinger film *Crude* offers a prime example (see Figure 6.2). After an initial teaser segment that sets up the conflict between the Chevron Corporation and scrappy Ecuadoran lawyer Pablo Fajardo, who has brought a class action lawsuit on behalf of hundreds of villagers who claim to have been harmed by the frequent oil spills in their ancestral lands, the film shows Fajardo on a boat traveling along the Amazon. The audience begins to overhear him speaking: "First of all, thank you for the welcome, thank you for having us," he says in Spanish. For the next 47 seconds, Fajardo is heard speaking to the villagers while they travel by boat and on foot to the modest community center where he is giving his talk, interleaving the travel

Figure 6.2 Interleaving of scenes in *Crude*

footage with the scene of his speech. Finally, things come briefly into sync as the film shows him speaking to them in person, but soon the next scene makes its visual appearance even as Fajardo continues speaking. By the time it is over, a mere 38 seconds of the 135-second speech have been played as verité.

This interleaving of scenes breaks time up into multiple layers and allows the audience to experience multiple moments at once, often being pulled forward into a new place/time while continuing to experience the "present" as well.[4] As interleaving increases in complexity and intensity, it comes to approach the frictionless experience of montage.

Use of the Present Tense

We started this chapter noting that documentaries seek to convince the audience that what is depicted onscreen *actually happened*, but the illusion is even more profound. Most documentaries posit that what happens onscreen is *happening right now*. This conceit of operating in the present tense is different from some other art forms. In literature, for instance, the past tense has remained dominant. (*It was a dark and stormy night . . .*) As readers become engulfed in a story, they convert the past into present in their own minds, conjuring up the action that seems to take on a life of its own, yet the actual words on the page fashion the scene at a realistic remove.

The experience of watching a film, however, is fundamentally present tense. As audience members watch and listen, the film takes over their senses in an absolute way as they react to the images in front of them. Even if a section of a fiction film is clearly marked as a flashback, an audience still experiences it in present tense as it washes over them. Most documentaries, even though they are by definition about events that occurred well prior to the moment they are viewed, subscribe to the same conceit.

Consider the title cards from the opening of Martha Shane and Lana Wilson's documentary *After Tiller:*

> 9 states allow third-trimester abortions without legal restrictions.

> These abortions account for fewer than 1% of all abortions performed in the United States . . . and there are only four known doctors who can do them.

At first glance this presentation seems utterly reasonable and transparent, but consider what the documentary is actually communicating:

> As of the completion of this film in November 2012, nine states allowed third-trimester abortions without legal restrictions.

> These abortions had accounted for fewer than 1 percent of all abortions performed in the United States . . . and there were only four known doctors who could do them.

The difference is significant. By placing the drama in the present tense, the film sets up the conditions for narrative storytelling, and for the dream state the film wishes to induce.

Another example from a film on a similar topic drives the point home and shows how present-tense title cards can be intercut with "present tense" verité footage for a seamless effect. In a scene from 2020's *The Fight*, which follows four civil rights cases prosecuted by the ACLU during the years of the Trump administration, we follow a court case in which the government sought to force a seventeen-year-old migrant girl detained by Immigration and Customs Enforcement to carry her child to term against her will. Ramping up the tension, a title card comes on the screen.

> In the state where Jane Doe is detained,
> abortion is illegal after 20 weeks.
>
> She is 15 weeks pregnant.

"Time is a big factor, we're racing against the clock," says ACLU lawyer Brigitte Amiri as the audience sees her furiously composing a legal argument on her laptop aboard a train. Another title card follows:

> Brigitte asks the DC court for an emergency injunction.

Through a car windshield we pull up at the Capital Hilton, when a final title card sets the stage for the showdown:

> The judge sets the hearing for 9am tomorrow.

In reality all of this took place in the past, but to set the film in the present tense is to fully engage its dramatic possibilities.

Documentaries will sometimes take great pains to keep this illusion alive. Near the end of *Lost in La Mancha*, which I edited for directors Keith Fulton and Lou Pepe, actor Jean Rouchfort has left the set of Terry Gilliam's ill-fated Dox Quixote adaptation on an emergency visit to see his doctor back in Paris, and the producers are at a loss for how to move forward with the rest of the film shoot. Cut to producer Bernard Bouix, who is seen nervously biting his nails in the production office and states, "I think there is no worse situation than not knowing anything. . . . Everyone is asking every day, 'What do we have to do? When are we going to restart?' And nobody's able to give an answer."

It looks as though Bouix has just been momentarily pulled away from his desk to make these comments, but in fact the interview was recorded nearly a year later. So how did the film maintain the illusion and get him to talk in the present tense? Looking carefully at the interview, one can tell that Bouix's first "is" ("everyone *is* asking every day") is actually a dubbed line and that his mouth clearly says, "was." This is only visible on a third or fourth viewing of the film and tends to go unnoticed by audiences. Following this, the line, "nobody's able to give an answer," which occurs offscreen, was changed from "nobody *was* able to give an answer" with some careful audio editing. (The "wa" part of "was" was removed, such that "nobody was" was convincingly morphed into "nobody's.") The shift from past tense to present tense is significant, because it keeps the audience locked into the verité action onscreen and undistracted by a back-and-forth toggling between past and present. The ethical calculation that we made in enacting this change went something along the lines of *The basic meaning of the quote remains identical; we've just changed the audience's orientation toward it*. Whether this is right or wrong is for the reader to judge, but the fact remains that such manipulations are not uncommon.

Another aspect of the bias toward present-tense orientation is seen in the common choice to avoid explicit date markers. Given the long gestation period for most documentaries those markers would make a film feel dated even upon its initial release, so it works to the filmmaker's advantage to place the film in an "eternal present," providing relative markers of time but not absolute ones. ("Four months later" yes; "April 2022" no.)

Even films that are firmly rooted in historical time take great liberties with their depiction of it. *The Fight*, for instance, deftly cuts between four legal cases in ways that strongly imply simultaneity. As the film approaches its climax, all four lawyers show up in the ACLU's New York City conference room, going through their "moots" (practice sessions where they are grilled by their colleagues) for *Garza v. Hargan*, *Ms. L v. ICE*, *Stone v. Trump*, and *Dept. of Commerce v. New York*. The four are shown together onscreen in a split-screen moment, and then back to back as they get ready for their final arguments in their respective hotel rooms. As they travel to their courtrooms the next day, the film cuts to Lee in San Diego, Brigitte in DC, Josh in Baltimore, and finally to Dale as he steps out of his ride onto the steps of the Supreme Court.

The effect is thrilling as it takes the collective tension and anticipation built up by each story and binds it together. Yet these actions took place at wildly different times. The opening arguments for *Garza v. Hargan*, for instance, were heard on October 18, 2017, while the *Ms. L v. ICE* arguments weren't heard until February 21, 2019, and the *Dept. of Commerce v. New York* case commenced on April 23, 2019. Thus, the actions in one square of the split screen took place as much as eighteen months apart from the actions of the next, and the powerful simultaneity of them all stepping out of their vehicles on the same day is an illusion (see Figure 6.3). This sequence is only possible, of course, if all mentions of absolute time (i.e., specific dates) are scrubbed clean.

Figure 6.3 Four lawyers seem to work simultaneously in *The Fight*

Notes

1. The implicit promise of any live broadcast of a sporting event is that the event is truly *live*. This is why it can be disconcerting to watch time-shifted segments shown in these broadcasts, such as when the coaches of NBA teams are interviewed about their team's performance in between ad breaks and the interview is then played a couple minutes later when the ad breaks conclude. One may briefly feel alarmed that the coach seems to be ignoring the action of the game to talk calmly to the interviewer when in fact time is operating a couple minutes apart in different sections of the screen.
2. This list owes a debt to Dai Vaughan's similar formulation in his book *For Documentary* (Berkeley: University of California Press, 1999), 68.
3. *Stray*, directed by Elizabeth Lo (Magnolia Pictures, 2020), 00:03:22.
4. Careful readers may note the similarity of this technique with the pre-lap, discussed in the previous chapter. In essence the interleaving of scenes amounts to an extreme version of the pre-lap, with the audio from the upcoming scene inserting itself long before its visual appearance.

7
Titles

In a scene from Julia Reichert and Steven Bognar's Netflix documentary *American Factory*, a man in a blue work shirt and safety glasses appears onscreen. A few moments after he begins speaking, a simple title graces the bottom portion of the screen (see Figure 7.1).[1]

ROB
FURNACE SUPERVISOR

On the surface, this "lower third" title card is utterly unremarkable: name on top, job title underneath. Indeed, titles would seem to be one of documentary film's least mysterious elements. Sitting in the bottom third of the screen (thus the *lower-third* moniker), they simply provide an efficient, nonintrusive way for a filmmaker to get across some basic information. Instead of having every subject announce themselves—"Hi, I'm Crystal Hernandez, and I'm a surgeon"—the titles do it for them. But scratch the surface and you'll find that lower-third titles are yet another element in the documentary film that should always be interrogated for meaning. Titles influence an audience's understanding of the images they support; they structure how an audience thinks about who the subjects are and how they relate to each other; they have powerful aesthetic value that can convey textural and tonal information; and they play a role in manipulating audience attention in precise and intentional ways.

How Documentaries Work. Jacob Bricca, Oxford University Press. © Oxford University Press 2023.
DOI: 10.1093/oso/9780197554104.003.0008

Figure 7.1 A lower-third title card in *American Factory*

Naming Characters

Most documentarians wish to focus their audience's attention on a just few key protagonists in order to build a story that audiences can follow. The first way they do this is by formally separating the participants in the film into primary characters and secondary ones. With every new person that appears with a title beneath them, a subtle instruction is given to the viewer: remember this one, for this person likely to reappear.

Secondary characters with no title cards can't just be shoved in front of the audience willy-nilly or else confusion about their role and identity may result. But it is astonishing how much information can be supplied to the audience via context alone. Often the supporting characters' importance is defined by their relationship to others or as symbols of an idea. For example, in an early scene from *American Factory*, the audience encounters a hall full of out-of-work job seekers listening to a pitch by an executive from the Chinese auto glass giant Fuyao, which opened its factory doors in 2014 at the site of a previously shuttered General Motors plant. None of the workers are identified because the multiplicity of anonymous, unnamed folks is the point of the scene: *People are really down and out here in Dayton, Ohio, for there are too many to name.*

It is rare to see someone identified with a lower-third title as a part of an opening montage. An unspoken assumption made by filmmakers states that identifying names at the beginning of the film may be counterproductive, because the filmmaker is trying to create a suggestive *impression*, not to actually dig into the meat of the story and start in on the main characters. For example, the opening of *RBG* consists of a brisk montage of fifteen clips over fifty-one seconds showing Washington, DC, monuments and statues as the audience hears audio soundbites from a number of outraged men ("a witch," "a monster," "one of the most vile human beings"). The men are never identified, because to do so would be to utterly overwhelm the viewer, who is just trying to keep up with the fast-paced comments. More importantly, naming them with title cards would signal that the comments *needed* this additional context in order to fulfill their function, when exactly the opposite is true. Instead, their purpose is to give a *general* aura to the protagonist, Ruth Bader Ginsberg (she reviled by her detractors) and to set up the overall audience expectations about the story (it's a classic David vs. Goliath tale.)

The precise naming conventions used in lower thirds are crucial. Is the audience introduced to the protagonists with their full name, or just their first name? What kind of attribution are they given? A traditional lower third in which the full name of the participant is used above a professional title delivers the unmistakable impression of a formal, sober voice. This instantly suggests that the audience's relationship with the participant is a professional rather than a personal one, and the audience gets to know the person in the same way they might meet someone at a conference or a public forum. (*"Hi, I'm Maggie Desai; I'm the IT director for Midland Supplies."*) This kind of attribution instantly lends status and legitimacy to the subject and to the documentary itself by taking on the kind of formality associated with serious journalism. Titles confer status, status confers authority, and the documentary gains authority from those it puts onscreen in its pursuit of evidence and facts.

In contrast, using a first name only and leaving out professional qualifications is part and parcel of a film with a more intimate tone. Take the 2019 Academy Award nominee *Minding the Gap*. These young men are introduced simply as Zack, Bing, and Keire. Ditto for the 2016 drama *The Bad Kids*, whose three main protagonists are known to the audience only as Joey, Jennifer, and Lee. The scenes in these films are highly personal ones: the camera silently witnesses moments of great domestic anguish and triumph. The unspoken assertion made by the films is that the audience can learn a great deal about the issues at hand (domestic violence, poverty) from its survivors, without need of experts. Thus, it follows that the titles would introduce them to the audience as if they were already on a first-name basis.

It is not unusual for a documentary to have a couple different templates for its titles, creating different categories that can helpfully convey information about what role the subjects play within the overall logic of the film. In *Precious Knowledge*, which chronicles the bitter fight to outlaw the teaching of Mexican American studies classes in the Tucson Unified School District, the three main student characters (all Latinx) are introduced with only their first names. The first letters of their names are in an Old English font of the kind popular in Chicano street culture (see Figures 7.2–7.4).

All of the teachers, administrators, and politicians, however, are given traditional formal titles in the clean, nondescript Optima font (see Figures 7.5–7.7).

Here the filmmakers want the audience's hearts with the students, and their heads with the adults, who seek to educate them and to do battle over the justifiability of the controversial academic program.

Conferring Legitimacy

If lower-third titles provide context and confer legitimacy, what does it mean when a filmmaker eschews them? The films of Frederick Wiseman provide a fascinating case study in the effect achieved when a director chooses to forgo all lower-third titles. A living

Figures 7.2–7.4 The lead student characters in *Precious Knowledge* introduced with only their first names

Figures 7.5–7.7 Teachers, administrators, and politicians introduced with their full names and titles in *Precious Knowledge*

documentary legend, Wiseman has been making films at the rate of one per year for over fifty years and has never once put a lower-third title in any of his films.

Wiseman's voice is often skeptical in its stance toward authority, especially in his earlier films. *High School* is a searing indictment of enforced conformity at a Philadelphia public high school. *Near Death* is an astonishing six-hour portrait of the futility of medical intervention at a Boston hospital. *Zoo* takes the audience inside Miami's Metro Zoo with a distinctly critical take on the ethical justifiability of keeping wild animals in captivity. This point of view is achieved through various means. Wiseman's rigorous method, which often involves filming in a single location of a public institution for an extended period of time, allows him to put institutional cultures under a microscope. He is uninterested in creating character portraits, which further focuses his audience's attention on the institution rather than the individual. His frequent use of extreme close-ups plays its part. But a crucial supporting role comes from the absence of identifying lower-third title cards.

In *Titicut Follies*, for instance, as the audience sees scenes play out among the patients and staff at the Bridgewater Massachusetts Correctional Institution, a psychiatric facility, they never learn the names or titles of anyone. In fact, the film never even shows an establishing shot of the building, and the name of the facility is not identified until the end credits roll.[2] The lack of quick comprehension increases the audience's level of curiosity, leading them to scrutinize the behavior of the subjects on a deeper level. Not only that, but it also takes away the authority that would otherwise be granted to the doctors and guards staffing the facility. They costume themselves in uniforms that are meant to *claim* authority, but without the quick understanding of their putative role, the audience is asked to look at everything differently.

What the audience is left with is a perspective that feels like a blank slate: a variety of human actors playing out roles and treating each other in particular ways, which the audience must observe closely in order to figure out who's who and what's going on. The staff, which treats its charges with a mixture of pity and contempt, seems at times

Figure 7.8 Lack of identifying titles making it hard to distinguish between guards and patients in *Titicut Follies*

to be just as "crazy" as the patients, who act strangely at times but often exhibit more humanity and common sense than their jailers (see Figure 7.8). Stripped of hierarchy by the film's approach, everyone becomes equal before Wiseman's camera.

If an absence of titles can be used to question authority, can those same lower thirds be used to actively buttress it? A close look at the series *Beyond Scared Straight*, which ran on A&E from 2011 to 2015, suggests that it can. Each episode shows a different group of juvenile delinquents forced to spend time with convicts in adult prisons as a way of teaching them to straighten up and fly right. This "tough love" approach is often hard to watch, with prison guards and inmates frequently taunting and shouting at the young teenagers. "This seemed overly abusive and horrifying without a lower third," said editor Mark S. Andrew, ACE, who worked on the show for four years. "Making sure that we identified the subject as someone who brought a loaded gun to school helped to solidify why he was in this program to begin with, and eliminated some thoughts of the program being

BAKARI, 15
Breaking & Entering / Theft

Figure 7.9 Lower-third titles in *Beyond Scared Straight*

too cruel." Indeed, a close look at the editing reveals that the lower third is often introduced precisely at the moment when the verbal harangues reach their maximum intensity, and is clearly designed to temper the audience's gut response with information that offers an implicit justification of the harsh treatment (see Figure 7.9).

Title cards are often used in other creative ways to nudge the viewer toward a particular interpretation of what they see in front of them. Julien Faraut's 2018 documentary *John McEnroe: In the Realm of Perfection* takes a single tennis match—the 1984 French Open final between John McEnroe and Ivan Lendl—and dissects it for hidden psychological implications. The match, which occurred when McEnroe was the world's highest ranked player, ended up being the beginning of the end of his career, and the film does everything it can to build it up as an epic. The film is peppered with titles that display the time of day and the elapsed time of the match as a way of consistently cutting forward in time to a new scene. All these titles appear in the same size font until the climax of the film—the moment at which McEnroe will face his ultimate test. Suddenly the figures appear significantly larger, heightening the audience's expectations and nudging them to understand the upcoming scene as particularly crucial to the story (see Figure 7.10).

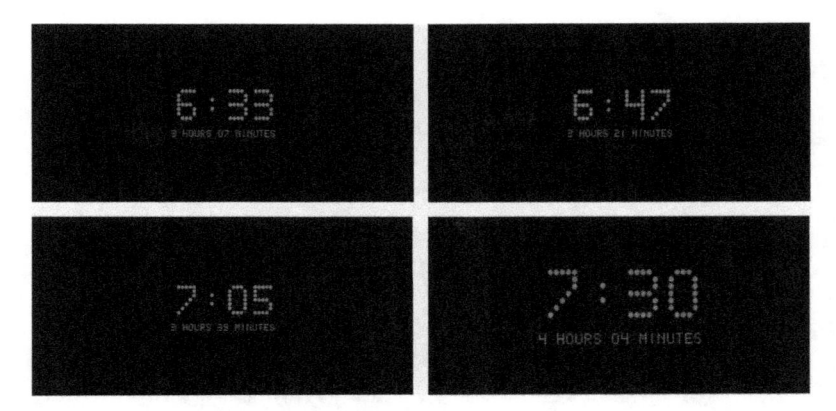

Figure 7.10 Onscreen titles in *John McEnroe: In the Realm of Perfection.* The final title appears directly prior to the scene in which McEnroe loses the match

Titles are also subject to the storytelling logic of each particular film. *Tiger King* introduces the audience to John Finlay as the husband of the titular character in Episode 1. He continues to be identified as such all the way through Episode 5, when their relationship turns sour. The moment of divorce is never precisely identified or explained, but in the logic of the storyline it occurs sometime between seventeen minutes into Episode 5, when he is still identified as "Joe's Husband," and four minutes into Episode 6, when he suddenly becomes "Joe's Ex-Husband" (see Figures 7.11 and 7.12). The interview in Episode 6 is the same one used in all the previous episodes, however, so it becomes clear to the astute observer that the earlier use of title is technically inaccurate since he was actually divorced when the interview took place. The title is true insofar as it connects to the ongoing logic of the *story* but is untrue as it relates to the actual conditions of production.

Look and Feel

The look and feel of titles (font choice, exact placement onscreen, animation or lack thereof) is never a neutral choice. Traditional

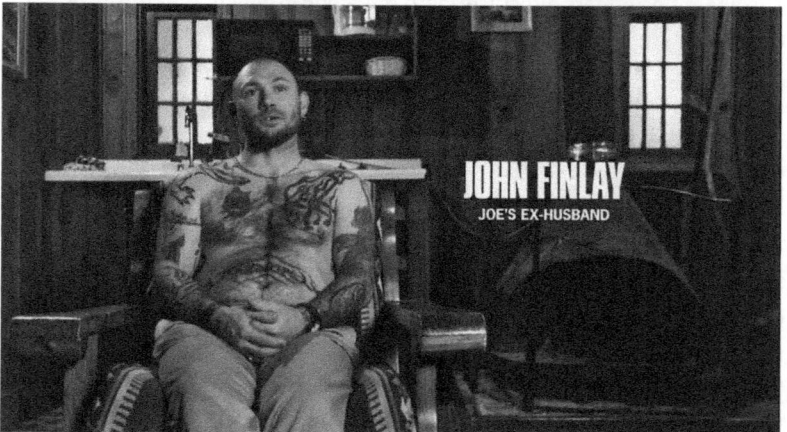

Figures 7.11 and 7.12 John Finlay instantly becoming "Joe's Ex-Husband" in *Tiger King: Murder, Mayhem and Madness*

conventions mandated that these titles stay strictly within the boundaries of the bottom third of the screen; however, many filmmakers now choose to simply place them wherever the title seems most aesthetically pleasing. Conversely, choosing a placement that breaks standard rules of composition can create its own subtle psychological effects. In the 2010 MTV series *If You Really Knew Me*, lower thirds were placed askew and off center to try to symbolize the division and acrimony between the different high school cliques portrayed in the show. Additionally, the font for the main title was

Figure 7.13 MTV's *If You Really Knew Me*

"distressed" with imperfections in the individual characters and a messy spray of ink around the edges (Figure 7.3).

While these were meant to stick out, the choice of font style in the 2019 documentary *Diego Maradona* was designed explicitly to fit in. The bulk of the film plays out in the 1980s and is composed entirely of archival footage from the era, so it has the telltale low-res feel of interlaced video played on the old-fashioned cathode ray tubes of the day. The film does not try to "clean up" the video but rather uses its texture as a mark of authenticity, and when titles come onscreen, they have exactly the resolution and the color cast of the archival video, in a font with a drop shadow treatment that could have come from the era. The match is so perfect, in fact, that it could easily be mistaken for belonging to the archival sources themselves (see Figure 7.14).

Looking through lower-third titles from earlier eras shows that they are just as prone to visual design trends as any other aspect of cinema. Just as shock zooms were ubiquitous in 1970s cinema, and *The Matrix* popularized the skip bleach method of intentionally misprocessing the film that lent it the dystopian green/gray feel that continues in many sci-fi films to this day, titles are a product of their era. "Thicker fonts like Arial Bold and Copperplate were popular in

Figure 7.14 Heavy drop shadow on the titles, perfectly matching the 1980s archival material in *Diego Maradona*

the early 2000s," recalls David Michael Maurer, ACE. "These days designers use thinner, modern fonts, and there are lighting effects added to create more luster." Their duration has also changed over the years. In the mid-1990s lower thirds would regularly be put onscreen for three to five seconds, where now one frequently encounters cards that are onscreen for under two seconds. This follows an overall trend toward more rapid cutting, placing demands on viewers to make quicker comprehension of onscreen text material.

Titles are also sometimes used to distract. As editor Jim Ruxin, ACE says of his work on television shows such as Big Tips Texas, Project Runway, and The Apprentice, "If the interview subject is compelling, simple text is mandated; if the material is weak, then you need to add interest." This use of graphics to draw attention to themselves can go even further, such that the animated title can become an intentional attempt to distract from problems of logic in the story itself. As Ruxin states, highly active or distracting animated titles may be "a sign of keeping the screen active and the viewer engaged in decoding the movement so as to disable their critical thinking. The audience is too busy to form a solid connection with the speaker or too busy to detect misleading or conflicting statements."

Subtitles

When director Bong Joon-Ho took the stage at the 2020 Academy Awards to accept the award for *Parasite* as Best International Feature Film, he remarked, "Once you overcome the one-inch-tall barrier of subtitles, you will be introduced to so many more amazing films." This was something of a watershed moment, as the Academy would also award Joon-Ho with the Best Directing award and *Parasite* with the Best Picture Oscar just a few moments later. Audiences worldwide have grown accustomed to international content reaching their shores in subtitled versions, but it was symbolically important for Americans to finally climb over this barrier as well. All but one of the nominees for Best Documentary Feature at the 2020 Academy Awards were completely or partially subtitled for American audiences, and Netflix and other streaming services have made Americans more and more comfortable with subtitles via the many international series that come with English subtitles as the default option.

Subtitles represent another layer of information that reaches the audience and their production involves numerous layers of decision-making by filmmakers about exactly how and what to translate. As David MacDougall notes, "Although the people in the film are speaking to each other, subtitles are one of the ways in which the filmmaker speaks to us."[3]

With subtitles, the precise meanings of the words can be sculpted to match the narrative and emotional needs of the film. Take this example from Lisa Molomot and Jeff Bemiss's 2020 documentary *Missing in Brooks County*, which I produced and edited, in which human rights activist Eddie Canales takes a call from an unnamed woman on the phone who is trying to locate her missing daughter. Note the subtle difference in Table 7.1 between the literal translation and the actual words used in the film.

As you can see, there is considerable creative license when it comes to the use of subtitles. There are several places where words in the original are eliminated in the subtitles for brevity. But there are also places where words never spoken in the original are added, such as when "Where did they enter?" is changed to "Where did they enter

Table 7.1 Subtitle translation for a scene from *Missing in Brooks County*

Original	Literal translation	Subtitle	Reason for change
¿Que tan grande era el grupo?	How large was the group?	How big was the group?	More colloquial
Eran diez personas.	There were ten people.	Ten people.	Shortened for brevity
Mi hija y el muchacho son pareja, y no conocíamos a nadie.	My daughter and the boy, they're a couple, and we didn't know anybody.	My daughter and her boyfriend went together, but they didn't know any of the others.	Corrected for clarity; makes the meaning more explicit
¿Donde entraron ellos? ¿Por donde entraron?	Where did they enter? From where did they enter?	Where did they enter the country?	Shortened for brevity; added "the country" to make it clear they're talking about someone crossing the border
Por el río.	From the river.	From the river.	[No change]
Es como que estaban en un pueblo, y entraron al río.	They were in a town and they entered by way of the river.	They came through a town and then crossed the river (Rio Grande).	Improved clarity; added "Rio Grande" to further solidify geography in the mind of the viewer
¿Y saben que ropa traían puesta o algo así?	Do you know what clothes they were wearing or anything like that?	Do you know what clothes they were wearing?	Shortened for brevity
No, no, no.	No, no, no.	No.	Shortened for brevity

the country?" There is also an important change in the third line: the literal meaning of "My daughter and the boy, they're a couple, and we didn't know anybody" could be quite confusing on its own, but when changed to "My daughter and her boyfriend went together, but they didn't know any of the others," it takes some of the implied meaning and makes it explicit so that the audience can understand the *intent* of the sentence rather than just its literal translation (see Figure 7.15).

A filmmaker can also emphasize words that would ordinarily go unnoticed by putting in a subtitle for a line of dialogue that is heard faintly in the distance or in passing. Or emphasis can be added by modifying the amount of time a subtitle rests on the screen. As

Figure 7.15 Subtitles helping to clarify the meaning of the words in *Missing in Brooks County*

David MacDougall notes, "The final subtitle of a scene will sometimes be treated . . . as a form of punctuation, or to foreshadow the content of the ensuing scene."[4] (We saw in Chapter 5 how this extra pause is often used in editing to achieve a similar effect.)

Conversely, entire sections can be left without any subtitles if it suits the intention of the scene. *Derrida*, a 2002 film profiling the French philosopher and social critic Jacques Derrida, portrays him as a fierce deconstructionist in every aspect of his life, refusing to let the awkwardness of filming go unremarked upon. ("I want . . . to remark on the completely artificial character of this situation," he says in a subtitled moment at the beginning of one interview. In another subtitled exchange he points out the presence of the cameras during one of his classes and quips, "We'll see what it's like to work . . . in the presence of these archiving machines.")[5] As the filmmakers follow him home and show him taking a phone call, they choose to play the scene without any subtitles at all. The point of the scene—to observe his behavior in a seemingly unguarded moment—is better accomplished by focusing more of the audience's attention on his actions rather than his words, since the conversation did not play into the narrative of the film.

Filmmakers must be careful with their creative license, however, for confusion can be an unintended consequence of a well-meaning substitution. The audience expects, for instance, that most extended utterances will carry a correspondingly long subtitle. Substituting a long sentence whose meaning can be successfully summarized with a simple onscreen "yes" can feel awkward and misleading, even when the substitution is accurate.[6]

For better or worse, subtitles do have the effect of emphasizing words over other nonverbal forms of communication and give the unspoken impression that the act of translation is an uncomplicated project. Languages are expressions of cultures, each of which has its own unique history, traditions, and customs, and sometimes there is simply no adequate translation for a phrase. "Hijo de puta!" someone may exclaim loudly in Castilian Spanish, and neither the literal translation ("Son of a whore!") nor a common substitution ("Son of a bitch!") gets close to describing what it means to impugn the sexual purity of another's family in traditionally Catholic Spain. As David MacDougall wisely notes, "Subtitles may induce in viewers a false sense of cultural affinity since they so unobtrusively and efficiently overcome the difficulties of translation. They may reinforce the impression that it is possible to know others without effort—that the whole world is inherently knowable and accessible."[7]

Notes

1. *American Factory*, directed by Julia Reichert and Steven Bognar (Higher Ground Productions, 2019), 00:24:47.
2. There is one shot of the exercise yard, but there are no shots of the outside of the building.
3. David MacDougall, *Transcultural Cinema* (Princeton, NJ: Princeton University Press, 1998), 174.
4. MacDougall, *Transcultural Cinema*, 172.
5. *Derrida*, directed by Kirby Dick and Amy Ziering (Jane Doe Films, 2002), 00:14:12 and 00:18:45.
6. MacDougall, *Transcultural Cinema*, 172.
7. MacDougall, *Transcultural Cinema*, 175.

8
Archival Material

Archival documents carry a special aura. Their status as evidence makes them seemingly unimpeachable and gives them a feeling of authenticity. The scratches and imperfections on a piece of old Super-8 or 16 mm film give a visceral sense of separation from the present day that instantly heightens a film's perceived genuineness and increases its ability to evoke nostalgia. Even the low resolution of VHS or Hi8 video now evokes a warm fuzzy feeling for some viewers who remember the 1980s and 1990s with fondness.

Yet one should be careful of these knee-jerk emotional reactions because of the multiple layers of intervention that go into the selection, manipulation, and presentation of a piece of archival material in a documentary. The markers of age shown by a piece of archival film, created by specks of dust rubbing against a film print as it moved through a projector at twenty-four frames per second, are today more accurately characterized as an optional stylistic choice than an inevitable marker of age. Those scratches can be removed by an old-fashioned "wet gate" telecine transfer, in which the film is submerged in perchloroethylene at the time of scanning to video, and further removed with digital technology. Or scratches can be accentuated in the picture grading process by adjusting the contrast, color tone, and sharpness of an image. In fact, it's debatable whether it is even possible to show any piece of old film footage in a neutral way. But the allure of authenticity that can be created with archival material that appears to "look its age" is impossible for many nonfiction filmmakers to resist.

How Documentaries Work. Jacob Bricca, Oxford University Press. © Oxford University Press 2023.
DOI: 10.1093/oso/9780197554104.003.0009

Archival Treatments

It has become increasingly common for a documentary to high-light the status of archival footage *as archival* by choosing to show not only the image itself, but also the sprocket holes to the sides of the frame as well, as in the recent music biopics *David Crosby: Remember My Name* (see Figure 8.1) and *Miles Davis: Birth of the Cool.* This is something that never would have been shown in the original presentation of the film in a theater or on a flatbed editing table, and was also never part of the telecine transfer to video, so it has no reason to exist except to highlight its status as something old and "authentic."

It is also becoming common practice to put the archival image inside a different visual context by shooting it on an era-appropriate device. This is done in the HBO doc series *McMillions*, for instance, when footage from 1995 is shown on an old Hitachi television sitting in a domestic setting with era-appropriate wood paneling in the background (see Figure 8.2). This is akin to putting a reenactment wrapping around the archival image, seeking to evoke the era that it comes from in addition to displaying the archival content itself.

Figure 8.1 Sprocket holes on the side of the frame in *David Crosby: Remember My Name*

Figure 8.2 Archival image placed inside of a 1980s Hitachi television set in *McMillions*

Ironically, these images are typically created by layering in the archival element as a *digital effect* composited onto the image of the old device rather than by actually running a video signal through it, so even the production of imagery meant to evoke old ways of doing things is done with the latest technology.

The same "picture within picture" idea is operative in the Netflix documentary *They'll Love Me When I'm Dead*, which tells the story of the making of Orson Welles's last film *The Other Side of the Wind*. The archival material is put inside television screens (for archival TV) and flatbed editing table screens (for film clips) frequently throughout the opening third of the film (see Figure 8.3).

Many documentaries go further than this. In Kirby Dick and Amy Ziering's *Outrage*, which documents the media's complicity in defending a heteronormative cultural environment over several decades, archival images from different sources are placed inside convincing-looking 35 mm contact sheets (see Figure 8.4). Later the documentary shows television images side by side. The animations are meant to evoke a "media moment"—a panoramic view across a generalized media landscape—and function as an updated version of the classic clicking-through-channels montage.

Figure 8.3 Archival image of Orson Welles digitally placed on the screen of a flatbed editing table in *They'll Love Me When I'm Dead*

Figure 8.4 Animated segment placing still images inside of 35 mm contact sheets in *Outrage*

Other documentaries will go so far as animate still images with artificial moving-picture scratch marks to make the images feel older or more authentic, as in Figure 8.5, an example from *Joan Jett: Bad Reputation*.

Figure 8.5 Scratch marks added to a still frame image in *Joan Jett: Bad Reputation*

Still other documentaries will use a contemporary still image shot by the documentary filmmakers *as archival*. In *The Kingmaker*, for instance, former First Lady of the Philippines Imelda Marcos is seen showing off thousands of legal documents, all cases leveled against her family for corruption and looting of state assets. At the close of the segment, an old-fashioned flashbulb pop is heard and a quick flash to white is seen. When the flash to white concludes, the audience is looking at the selfsame still frame of Marcos standing amid the sea of documents, as if it were one more archival still (see Figure 8.6). This is perhaps the rawest example of trying to extract the aesthetic *essence* from archival material and put it to work on other types of footage. The still photo was taken by the crew for *this* 2019 film documentary, but the flashbulb pop is a sound from a technology that has not been in use for at least a half century. Perhaps more than anything, this work succeeds in making the documentary *feel like a movie* because it is borrowing so heavily from fiction film conventions and clichés.

Figure 8.6 Photograph taken by the film crew and used as an archival document in *The Kingmaker*

Manipulation of Documents and Newspaper Assets

When used in a documentary, an archival document helps to tell a story. The court document or autopsy report may have simply been a *record* (a flat fact, a summary of information) before it took its place onscreen, but its inclusion in the film turns it into an instrument of the rhetorical and argumentative structure of the documentary. Indeed, it is the forward-moving, narrative-driven storytelling needs of the production that turn most shots of documents into quickly digested moments of focused meaning. To facilitate this quick crushing/juicing of meaning, there is almost always some help given to steering the audience's attention toward the elements that are germane to the argument. A soft vignetting (as seen in Figure 8.7) is perhaps the subtlest form of this technique. But it is not at all uncommon for the document itself to be altered from its original form. "I've worked on films about court cases where we've added a name to the beginning of a piece of text to identify the speaker that might not have been there on the original court document,"

Figure 8.7 A newspaper story as it appears in *Tiger King*

Figure 8.8 Original newspaper story from *The Tampa Tribune*, December 9, 1997

says editor Helen Kearns, ACE. "Other times we rearrange the formatting." The result is a partially manipulated, partially authentic document that does not clarify where the line between the two is drawn. The audience, rushed along by the pacing and forced to make quick work of the images, doesn't have the slack to discern these kinds of manipulations. "I think most of the time when you see a document come onscreen, you're just focused on paying attention to whatever that piece of information is that's being conveyed," continues Kearns. "You're not necessarily thinking about what's missing or how that piece of information came to you or what else could have been there."

A case in point is the newspaper clippings shown in *Tiger King: Murder, Mayhem, and Madness*. The images appear at first glance to be shots of physical documents, for the audience can see the texture of the fibers in the newsprint (see Figure 8.7). A closer look reveals something that more resembles heavy card stock, as if we are looking at a reprint of the original story. In fact, neither interpretation is correct: it is computer generated, and it is a manipulated version of the original story.[1] Carefully compare the original story in Figure 8.8 with the version in *Tiger King* (Figure 8.7) and you will see that two attention-grabbing pictures to the left of the headline in the original have been eliminated and replaced with text-only stories from further down the page. This draws attention directly to the story and eliminates distraction.

A similarly subtle manipulation can be seen in Amy Ziering and Kirby Dick's *On The Record*, which features on-camera interviews with women who publicly accuse hip-hop mogul Russell Simmons of rape. In that film, the photo credit and social media buttons that appeared in the original online version of a *New York Times* story about Harvey Weinstein (see Figure 8.9) have been scrubbed out (Figure 8.10). The hyperlink to Harvey Weinstein's name in the story has also been removed.

This is just the tip of the iceberg for visual manipulations. As the second episode of *Tiger King* winds down we find a moment in which the contents of a headline have been changed. As the show teases Episode 3 with breathless accusations of foul play related to the death of Carole Baskin's husband—"She's got a missing husband that's supposedly buried on her property!"—a "whoosh" sound is heard and the graphic in Figure 8.11 appears on the screen. The actual story looked like Figure 8.12.

Note that the usual rearrangement of elements has been performed in order to focus audience attention, but the content of the headline has also been changed from the cleverly alliterative (but too complex) "Missing millionaire a mystery to many" to a short and to-the-point "Millionaire's disappearance." Savvy newspaper readers

Figure 8.9 Original *New York Times* story with caption, photo credit, social media buttons, and clickable link, from October 5, 2017

Figure 8.10 The *New York Times* story as it appears in *On the Record*, with photo credit, social media buttons, and Weinstein hyperlink removed

DAY, SEPTEMBER 19, 1997

Millionaire's disappearance

■ Authorities think Jack Donald

Figure 8.11 A *Tampa Bay Times* story as it appears in *Tiger King*

48 TIMES ■ FRIDAY SEPTEMBER 19, 1997

LOCAL NEWS

Missing millionaire a mystery to many

■ Authorities think Jack Donald Lewis may be in Costa Rica but don't know whether he was taken or went there on his own.

By DAVID KARP and ERIKA D. PETERMAN
Times Staff Writers

TAMPA — On the morning millionaire Jack Donald Lewis disappeared, he was wearing a $1 T-shirt from Kmart and blue jeans bought at a yard sale. He left behind an 8-year-old Dodge van with a broken window and battered grill. He also left behind Wildlife on

his wife's urging, but did not return for follow-up visits, she said. He also told her several times he wanted a divorce, but she said he wasn't serious.

"It has been very, very difficult," Carole Lewis said. "It's what you both love and hate about him. I love that free spirit. He could just completely do something way, way out."

He's been his own man all his life, boot-strapping himself from Depression-era childhood to financial success through trucking and real estate.

Lewis was born in Dade City to a single mother of three, who sold fresh bread and worked as a seamstress. In high school, he held sev-

Don Lewis is the owner of a 40-acre wildlife sanctuary in Hillsborough County.

Handout photo

Figure 8.12 The original *Tampa Bay Times* story from September 19, 1997

would likely surmise that something was amiss with such a skimpy headline, but because it appears onscreen for less than two seconds it is virtually impossible for the audience to look at it long enough to register an objection.

Lest you think all of this is new, let's travel over forty-five years back in time to *Harlan County U.S.A.*, the masterful Barbara Kopple film that won the Academy Award for Best Documentary in 1976. The technology was different, but the effect was the same. Look at the difference between the original page 1 *New York Times* headline about the murder of United Mine Workers president Joseph Yablonski versus its representation in the film (Figures 8.13 and 8.14). In the

Figure 8.13 A *New York Times* article as it appears in *Harlan County U.S.A.*

Figure 8.14 The original article as it appeared in the *New York Times* on January 6, 1970

original, the headline appears well below the top of the page, dwarfed under a huge picture of Senator and Mrs. Edward M. Kennedy from an unrelated story. In the film, however, it sits directly under the masthead. What's more, a picture of Yablonski that never appeared on the front page has now been plopped into the story.

Savvy observers would note that the whole graphic has a "cut and paste" quality to it, but the forward momentum of the drama of the film and its short duration on the screen keep most viewers from paying much notice.

Historical Shorthand

Another thing to note about archival images is the loss of meaning they sometimes endure due to overuse. Certain images have now become so iconic as to lose almost all connection to their actual origin and instead refer to a kind of CliffsNotes version of history. In the United States, images of confetti-strewn parades and sailors getting off boats now stand in for a generalized "end of World War II" feeling, and protestors holding anti–Vietnam War signs stand in for the late 1960s. You can probably make up images in your own head for things like the Roaring Twenties and the Depression. Indeed, this is often their intended function in a documentary: an easy way for the film to instantly call up a large host of associations with two or three quick shots that situate a particular story in "history," gaining resonance by association. Sophisticated documentary filmmakers will use such images to build deeper portraits and problematize those images, but in lesser films the meanings delivered are superficial.

Documentary editors can themselves be surprised at what they find when they search beyond the "greatest hits" of an archive. Note editor Aaron Wickenden's experience working on the documentary *The Trials of Muhammad Ali.*

Ali is a public figure whose life is iconic. And yet a lot of those iconic moments have become sort of boiled down, whether it's a phrase that Ali said or a moment from a win in the boxing ring. Those become the most requested items from an archive, and the archives know that these are the "greatest hit" moments, so those go on the short reels and the process feeds on itself. Since we had access to the *full* archive and we had time to study it, it was fascinating to see the raw, extended moments. To be able to sit and watch the moment after the one when he says, "I am the greatest," when he continues and says, "I know God, I know the real God." That phrase became really important for the story we were trying to tell about his evolving belief system and helped us get out of the simplistic associations most people had.

The other, rarely acknowledged factor in the use of archival images is that those original images come with their own baggage. "One of the biggest errors I see people making with archival when they're first working with it is they're not thinking enough about the authorship that's embedded in the material," says filmmaker Penny Lane. "You need to understand and acknowledge and deal with the fact that that image was *authored* by somebody and has its own complicated point of view." Lane does this memorably in her 2016 film *Nuts!*, a quirky biography of the eccentric Dr. John Romulus Brinkley, a man who built a small empire with an "miracle cure" for impotence and a million-watt radio station in the 1920s. The film includes several excerpts from a biography called *The Life of a Man* penned by Clement Wood. The film at first quotes the book without question as it builds Brinkley up as a respectable individual, but later reveals that the book was essentially authored by Brinkley himself by paying Wood to put his name on a series of dictated statements. Thus, the film leads the audience through the same feeling of being duped that hundreds of Brinkley's own patients experienced, showing that stories previously presented as fact were actually fiction. "The idea that I was able to trade on the perceived 'authenticity' and uninterrogated authority of archival material with the use of that book was probably the biggest tool I had in my toolbox for *Nuts!*," says Lane.

Note

1. The practice of using computer-controlled cameras to perform precise moves over a physical copy of a newspaper is now a relic of the past, for the effect is cheaper to accomplish digitally in a fully computer-generated simulation. The digital process also allows easier manipulation of the documents.

9
Sound

Did you see that new documentary about Billie Eilish?
I don't mind viewing on a laptop, but I'd really rather see it in a theater.
I watched the whole eight episodes in one go.

See. View. Watch. When we talk about documentaries, we almost always speak in terms of visuals. This is understandable but unfortunate, because so much of the meaning of documentaries is contained in what we *hear*. An object doesn't just make a sound, it makes a *particular* sound in conjunction with myriad other sounds to build an environment that has an enormous influence on our emotions. As sound designer Peter Albrechtsen notes:

> If the cinematic moment is very quiet, we become very quiet. If we hear sudden eruptions of sound, we become uneasy. If we hear small, delicate sounds in the background, we feel that it's an intimate place to be. Sound has an enormous influence on our emotional perception of a scene.

It does this in part because humans perceive a tight bond between an object and the sound it produces. Thus, we hear the sound of wind by its movement through trees and we can tell people are entering the next room because their shoes make contact with the wooden floor. These expectations are exploited by documentary sound designers, who break up the sound of every scene into different elements that they manipulate independently. The background ambience may be soothing or grating, whisper quiet or quite loud, and this may have little to do with what was actually recorded in the moment. The objects that make noise have also been given a particular valence depending on the scene's intended emotional content and may have been altered or replaced in postproduction. Nearly everything an audience hears in a documentary has likely been significantly tweaked in postproduction.

This represents a shift from the way documentary sound was treated forty to fifty years ago. As the digital audio revolution swept through every section of the entertainment industry (live theater, film, television, music), it also gave innovative options to filmmakers. Audio tracks that once would have been unusable can now be included because of sophisticated audio-filtering and noise reduction technology. A densely layered soundtrack is available to nearly every filmmaker, not just those with the budget for a lengthy and expensive mix on a large soundstage. As Dolby engineer Robert Warren stated at the time of the release of 5.1 channel digital surround sound in the early 1990s, "The design, technical considerations, and specifications that [go] into the digital sound track . . . provide a medium that theoretically has no limitation."[1]

For better or worse, this has also opened the door to more and more extensive and sophisticated transformations and manipulations of recorded sound. In the documentary community, it is usually considered unethical to perform extensive visual effects on verité material; however, there are fewer sanctions placed on the embellishment of the soundtrack. While documentary sound editors place a premium on having access to the original sounds to work with, it is common practice to engage in extensive filtering and editing. By the time the mix is completed, sounds are so transformed that the difference between manipulating an original sound and inserting a new sound from another source may be somewhat academic.

Sweetening

The effects of this sound "sweetening" are profound. In the opening two minutes of *The Edge of Democracy*, Brazil's president, Luis Inácio

Lula da Silva, is seen walking down a hallway as he is led away to jail on corruption charges. Watching the picture without sound, it looks like a relatively calm and orderly affair. But the soundtrack tells a different story. The din of chanting protesters dies down from the previous scene only to be replaced by a shrill police siren as a reporter's voice, inserted from elsewhere, says, "Many patrol cars, many police vehicles are approaching." With these embellishments, the images of da Silva walking down the hall take on a new urgency. Somehow the hallway now seems more densely packed, and the shaky camera work feels more spontaneous.

The subtle effect of a seemingly small mixing choice can be profound, as in a scene in *Minding the Gap*. Kiere is one of three teenage boys growing up with abusive fathers in Rockford, Illinois; a significant aspect of his story is his slow climb out of poverty and he begins the film as a restaurant dishwasher who wants to find a way to move out of minimum wage work. As he arrives home and turns into the driveway in his beat-up sedan, the audio track contains the unmistakable squeal of a timing belt in need of repair, drawing attention to the poor condition of the car. "The sound mixer was used to taking things like that out," said director Bing Liu, "but I told them to play it up instead." With this emphasis, a damaged hubcap on one of the wheels of the car that might have gone unnoticed is now profoundly visible. Again, one small embellishment of sound works in an organic way to draw attention to something in the frame that helps deepen the characters and tell the story.[2]

Sound also instantly conveys a sense of what the offscreen space contains, and recent advances in digital technology have led film theoretician Mary Ann Doane to conclude that it has fundamentally shifted the purpose of the *picture* in contemporary cinema. "Sound design has not just achieved an equal status with the image," she says. "It has in fact surpassed it."[3] She argues that the trend away from a strict "wide to close" editing pattern in films is due in part to the vastly increased fidelity of the soundtrack. Whereas it was traditionally incumbent upon a picture editor to show a wide shot of the full environment to place the audience in space and define the geography, the sound field is now so rich that it can fulfill this function on its own, making it more and more common for editors to begin scenes with close-ups rather than wide shots and sometimes to do without wide shots altogether.[4]

It is also not uncommon to have extra reverb added in post on a documentary to change the perceived size of a particular space. In the opening moments of Penny Lane's *Hail Satan?* a member of the so-called Satanic Temple, a group whose activities lie somewhere between extreme satire and serious political engagement, gives an address in front of a government building in Florida. As he speaks into a reporter's microphone his voice sounds amplified as if it is coming from a large speaker somewhere and is bouncing off the concrete walls (see Figure 9.1). With the sweetened sound, it looks more like someone giving a serious speech and less like a small cluster of incredulous journalists following around a guy with a huge set of horns strapped to his head. The space feels larger, his words more important.

Figure 9.1 A press conference's audio is amplified in *Hail Satan?*

Foley

For foley work (the recording of footsteps and the like), the process is carried out similarly to the one employed in fiction films. A spotting session is created by the sound designer after having talked extensively with the director to identify the sonic intentions of every scene, including which sounds need embellishment with foley. The only difference is in style. "In fiction films, you can flash foley a bit more," says Peter Albrechtsen.

> I was working on a fantasy film called *Valhalla* about Nordic gods which had all these enormous visceral effects with the earth shaking on every step they took. In that kind of film, foley is extremely powerful and in your face, whereas it tends to be just the opposite in documentary because the audience is not supposed to notice the effect.

Thus, while foley is used liberally in documentaries, it tends to follow a different aesthetic. Rather than the clean, clear, "larger than life" sound of footsteps or body blows in a fiction film, it is placed lower in the mix and sometimes recorded intentionally off-mic so that it sounds less perfect and draws less attention to itself.

A case in point comes in a scene from the film *Forget Me Not*, which was mixed by Albrechtsen and directed by Sun Hee Engelstoft, about a shelter for unwed mothers in South Korea. Because of the strong social stigma attached to having children out of wedlock, most of the teenage mothers in the film will end up giving their young babies up for adoption to wealthy families; the film documents the agonizing scenes of separation when the mothers say goodbye to their children forever. The film's style is restrained and quiet, with music used only sparingly. Thus, says Albrechtsen, foley had to be recorded with extreme restraint and had to match the sometimes-rough production sound that was used in the rest of the film. "We experimented a lot with placing microphones in 'bad' positions, so it recorded with 'bad' acoustics to make it sound natural," says Albrechtsen. The result includes small moments like one in which the head of the shelter asks A. what she will do with her child. (All of the girls in the film are given pseudonyms and have their faces blurred.) A. hesitates, sitting with her child in her lap, patting its tummy. The sound of her hand on the soft cloth of the swaddling towel, which was not picked up by the microphone in the original recording, is softly audible in the mix. This subtle highlighting of the touch of a mother to her child would never be picked out by the audience as a postproduction effect, but it amplifies the overall feeling of connection between the two that is at the heart of the film's point of view.

Sound can be used to achieve the opposite effect as well, serving to make a scene feel cold and harsh. In an early reenactment scene in *Tell Me Who I Am*, Alex Lewis recounts the experience of waking up after surviving a serious auto accident with no memory whatsoever of his previous life. His brother, his parents, their dog, their house: all of it is new to him. "I'm coming at this with nothing," he says. He literally does not know who he is. A harsh crack is heard, followed by a violent cutting/crunching noise. In jittery, out-of-focus shots that feel queasy because of their sickly yellow tint, Alex's mother is preparing breakfast: a soft-boiled egg has been whacked open and cut in two and a piece of toast is quickly jolted from a toast holder and buttered with a rough noise that sounds like sandpaper on cardboard as the knife scrapes bits of char off the bread (see Figure 9.2). These sounds attach a sense of arbitrary violence to an otherwise unremarkable action and reflect Alex's state of mind as he encounters the rituals of everyday life as overwhelming. For someone with no

Figure 9.2 A soft-boiled egg about to be cracked open in *Tell Me Who I Am*

memories, the film is saying, the activities of one's home life can be as frightening as anything out of a horror movie.

Those sounds, according to the film's rerecording mixer George Foulgham, were created from layers of a half dozen or more sounds for each of the actions.

> The sound recordist did some excellent recording on location. Then the sound editors embellished it, so the cracking of the egg was layered with several different types of sound to give it depth. And then when I mixed it, I picked and chose which ones worked together, so that one sound didn't cloud another. And although it's working over only a split-second of time, you've got to make sure that it's absolutely correct before you can move on because getting the egg right then affects the toast, and then that affects the stirring of the spoon. So in itself the nine-second scene has its own little arc.

A similarly painstaking attention to detail was applied to the sounds of marathoners running trials in the feature documentary *Breaking2*, which chronicles the attempt by a cadre of top-notch athletic trainers to apply their protocols to three different runners attempting to run a full marathon in under two hours. As a pack of runners rounds a turn on a track at high speed, a full-bodied, supple, yet crisp sound is heard that makes the runners appear like they're moving even faster than they are (see Figure 9.3). Listening to rerecording mixer Karol Urban, CAS MPSE discuss the approach she took, one realizes the extraordinary effort applied to the most minute detail of this sound.

> There was a low abstract element, an airy motion element, and a literal footstep element. Panning the abstract element around the literal element using divergence, I gave the natural-sounding element a grounded center. I blended the sound with a mid- and rear-returning medium- and long-tailed reverb and rolled off some of the higher frequencies in the airy element. I balanced them to create a sound that leaned natural but had a subjective intensity and added to the sense of anxiety and speed.

Figure 9.3 Runners rounding a turn in *Breaking2*

Foley can also be applied to actions that do not actually make noise. The supple, surprisingly emotional sounds of water in *My Octopus Teacher* are a fascinating lesson in the power of sound to supply visceral aural information. Shot primarily underwater in a sea kelp forest in South Africa, the film tells the story of the emotional bond between Craig Foster and an octopus over the course of a year. The motions of the octopus are given texture and emotionality with gentle sloshing and burbling of water; with every move that the octopus makes, a soothing water sound can be heard. The touch of the octopus's suction cups on Foster's hand are also given a foley effect. None of this was ever actually heard by anyone because these actions cannot be heard by human ears underwater. But the embellishment with sound gives them a powerful emotional effect.

Time and Space

Sound also plays a crucial element in constructing the audience's perception of time. As Albrechtsen notes:

> If the ambience in the background changes but there are still some other sounds that continue, then we feel that there's been a time jump.

If *everything* changes, then you feel there's also a location jump. We use these cues to create the internal time and geography of every sequence. Sound mixers often refer to this as a "reset" or a "bump."

Lauren Greenfield's *The Kingmaker*, which Albrechtsen also worked on, provides a perfect example of this phenomenon. In the opening moments of the film, Imelda Marcos points out landmarks from her perch on a luxury bus seat and the film cuts to what she sees. "When I see Manila, I feel so depressed and sad," she says as she points to residents living in small tents outside. The film cuts back to Marcos, and she then turns her gaze to the Malacañang Presidential Palace and says, "This is the palace." What happens next is subtle but crucial, for as the film again cuts back to Marcos in her seat there is a noticeable shift in the background ambience, signaling a jump forward in time before she continues speaking. Without the shift in ambience, her continuing dialogue—"I miss the clout of being First Lady"—would be perceived as a *continuation* of the same scene; but because the film intends to keep things moving swiftly forward, it arbitrarily divides the scene in two. This turns a single forty-three-second scene into one scene of twenty-eight seconds followed by another of fifteen seconds, which is in keeping with the aggressive pace of the beginning of the film. As shown in Figure 9.4, the verbal content and duration of the action has not changed, but the sequence now feels punchier and livelier because it is (subtly, subconsciously) experienced as *two* moments in time rather than one.

Sound is also commonly used to alter an audience's understanding of physical geography and of one action's physical proximity to another. In my 2006 documentary *Indies under Fire: The Battle for the American Bookstore*, irate protesters gather outside the grand opening of a new Borders bookstore in Santa Cruz, California, upset that the massive chain, which had well over three hundred stores at the time, was threatening their beloved local bookseller two blocks away. After hearing their chants, the film cuts inside the store to find Borders store manager Kris Arnett planted near the window looking out on the scene. In point of fact, the sound from the protests did not penetrate the thick glass of the windows, but it can clearly be heard

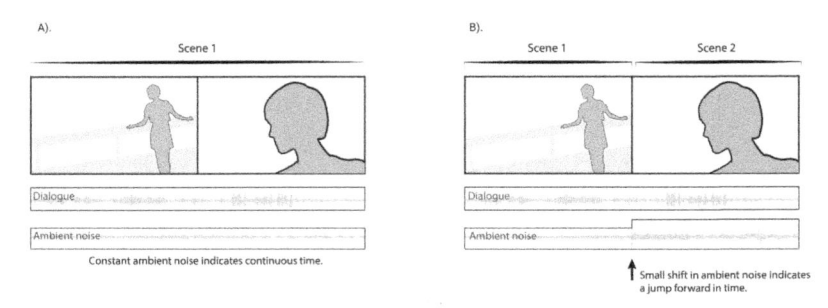

Figure 9.4 A shift in background noise alters the audience's perception of time

Illustration by Kaylah Rasmussen.

in the film, with little bits of dialogue discernible. This subtle embellishment completely changes the character of the scene, for now the conflict between Arnett and the protesters is viscerally present. The audience sees her standing at the window and perceives her to be not only seeing them, but also hearing their cries.

This same technique is used in *Honeyland*. The film captures the conflict between Hatidze Muratova, a beekeeper who lives with her mother in a rural Macedonian village, and a family who arrives to try to make a go of beekeeping themselves but follows unsustainable practices that diminish the long-term viability of everyone's hives. In one scene, the audience sees Muratova performing the delicate operation of extracting the honey from one of her hives as she makes her familiar yelping sound, calling out loudly to no one in particular. The film then cuts to the patriarch of the visiting family sitting in his truck, repairing his own beekeeping equipment, and the audience can hear Muratova's yelping faintly in the background as if it's coming from over the hill. The father turns his head as if he's hearing something, and then continues on with his work. In fact, these two scenes were shot months apart; but the overlapping sound connects the two protagonists, linking their fates together as well as the supposed geography between them.

In another scene, the audience sees the father hammering some pieces of scrap metal onto his roof to fix a leak; the hammering can then be faintly heard in the background over a shot of Muratova back in her hut, feeding her mother. While Muratova makes no acknowledgment of the sound, the fact that the two scenes (which, again, took place at completely different times) are placed in sonic proximity increases the audience's perception of their geographical and thematic proximity.

Framing Presence with Sound: *The Cave* and *For Sama*

The sound choices made in documentaries do not exist in a vacuum; they are inextricably linked to each film's framing of presence, and to its overall stylistic and institutional identity. Two Syrian civil war documentaries nominated for Best Documentary at the 2020 Academy Awards offer an extraordinary opportunity for comparison. Both *The Cave* and *For Sama* feature doctors running underground hospitals in cities under siege, but their approach to sound editing and mixing couldn't be more different.

The premise of *The Cave* is to capture life inside a hospital on the outskirts of Damascus, which has been set up underground because of the increased level of safety it provides given the ongoing mortar attacks. Dr. Amani Ballour is the protagonist, a young female doctor running the hospital who grows increasingly weary as the extent of the injuries inflicted by the Syrian and Russian forces intensifies (see Figure 9.5). In *For Sama*, the protagonist is a young female journalist named Waad Al-Kateab, whose husband Hamza is a doctor who runs a similar underground operation in Aleppo (see Figure 9.6). The shooting conditions were extremely challenging on both films, and the resulting production sound was correspondingly rough. (*The Cave* sound designer Peter Albrechtsen called the original sound he received "awful.")

Here is where the similarities between the two films end. *The Cave* fashions itself as a high-end documentary with art cinema touches. Produced by Danish Documentary—which calls itself "an international key player in the world of high-end cinematic documentary films"—with significant financing from National Geographic

Figure 9.5 Dr. Amani Ballour in *The Cave*

Figure 9.6 Waad Al-Kataeb in *For Sama*

Documentary Films, its opening sequence uses visual effects to take the audience from the top floor of a Damascus high-rise building all the way underground in a single, slowly descending shot. "I was against using a 'journalistic' opening," said director Feras Fayyad. "It was a metaphoric opening with artifacts from Judaism, Christianity, and Islamism embedded in the cracks of the building to show that this country has been a place for multiple religions all built over each other through history." (As visual effects supervisor Chadi Abo said, "[The opening] was very arty. It was never meant to be real.") The film had four cinematographers, three of whom were sometimes rolling at the same time and had to be digitally removed from each other's shots to protect their anonymity, and it offers its audience extraordinary access to its protagonist and the injured who are carted into the hospital.

For Sama, by contrast, was produced by the News and Current Affairs division of Channel 4 in the UK, which calls itself "the home of challenging investigative journalism." "This is a news department," said *For Sama* rerecording mixer Jez Spencer, "so you can't put anything in the film that could be interpreted as misleading the public." Visual effects were verboten, and the entire film plays as "realist." There is one primary cinematographer, Waad Al-Kateab, who narrates the film to her young daughter Sama (thus the title) and presents things from a first-person, participatory point of view.

The approach to sound in each film is remarkably different. Laboring for over a year on the sound, *The Cave*'s sound designer, Peter Albrechtsen, and his team threw away all the original sound except for the dialogue tracks and went to work recreating the sonic environment from scratch. Every footstep of the doctors as they shuffled down the halls, every beeping medical device, every scuffling wheel from a hospital gurney, was recorded or acquired in postproduction. The goal, as stated by director Feras Fayyad, who was himself once tortured by Syrian forces and lived through many years of the war, was to "hear it as a Syrian who has experienced multiple bombings over many years."

> Every single sound is bigger for me that what you might hear yourself. It's the sound of being three floors underground and there's no light so you don't know the day from the night. The warplane is a few miles away from you, but you feel that it's right on top of you. When the bomb hits, it feels like it's right next to you even though it may be far away.

Historical accuracy was important to *The Cave*'s filmmakers, with extensive research given to finding recordings of the precise models of military equipment that were being used by the Syrian and Russian forces at the time; but since the goal was immersion and subjectivity and they were starting with a blank slate, anything was fair game.

The result is a lush and detailed sonic experience that has more in common with the incredible soundscapes of *Saving Private Ryan* than with many other documentaries. The full capabilities of the Dolby Atmos platform are on display with sounds emanating from above, behind, in front of, and to the left and right of the viewer. Even listening to the film in plain stereo, the stereo separation (i.e., how much specificity the viewer can discern about the exact location of a particular sound) is often extraordinary, and the film makes full use of every sector of the frequency spectrum. Mortar attacks often arrive with a deep bass element that is rounded out by the higher frequencies of the debris scatter that can also be heard, often pushing the limits of what would actually be possible to hear in a location several feet underground. The audio is indeed traumatizing, especially when accompanied by the sometimes-dissonant musical score, but it is also expansive and resonant. The audience can hear every horrifying detail.

The raw sound recorded for *For Sama* was equally rough. It was frequently distorted and sourced almost entirely from the single camera mic on Waad Al-Kateab's camera. But instead of discarding most of the sound and starting from scratch, the *For Sama* crew simply went to work putting the tracks to use. This was partly a result of the rules of journalism as practiced by the News and Current Affairs division of Channel 4. According to Spencer, adding in sounds that did not emanate from the production tracks was off the table: no searching through sound effects libraries, no adding in extra explosions taken from another scene to augment the emotions of a particular moment.

The first thing one notices is the difference in stereo separation. Whereas *The Cave* uses the stereo field liberally, *For Sama* sets nearly all its sounds in the original mono. What one hears is generally confined to the way that the *camera* perceived the incoming noises, as opposed to an interpretation of what the *protagonists* may have heard. For instance, when Al-Kateab ventures outside, she encounters a man on a motor scooter drive from right to left across the screen, but its sound comes from the center throughout the duration of the shot. The frequency spectrum is also generally more restricted. A mortar attack arrives in one of the first scenes of the film and is heard powerfully in the background.[5] It registers higher in a frequency spectrum than similar attacks in *The Cave*—less resonant, more abrasive—and is again heard through both speakers equally. It does not have the same richness or specificity of the sounds in *The Cave*, but gains power from its claim to a more credible representation of the recording that was possible at the time. The jolts and jostling of the camera mic against the side of the camera are heard frequently throughout the film, reminding the audience of the act of filming.

As each film builds up to its climax, both films feature a breaking-point scene when a large mortar attack arrives and the characters are pushed to abandon their hospitals. In *The Cave*, this is rendered with a volume level and overall level of aural chaos that is larger than before but stays firmly within the overall parameters of the sonic palette that has been established for the film: rich and resonant. In *For Sama*, the attack results in a sustained blast of extremely overmodulated sound—pure crackling noise with very little detail—that evidences the sound overwhelming the microphone's ability to faithfully record it. Thus, whereas *The Cave* posits an imagined observer with extraordinary powers of perception, able to hear fine detail with no restrictions (consistent with its high-end production values and observational framing), *For Sama* posits its world as closely connected to the camera in the hands of its director and is frequently self-referential, which is consistent with its participatory framing and hard news institutional context.

However, it would be a mistake to simply mark *The Cave* as more "Hollywood" and *For Sama* as more "realistic." For instance, Spencer made full use of audio equalization tools in mixing a mortar attack in *For Sama*.

> I took that sound and ran it through a subharmonic synthesizer, be-
> cause without punching through that sub, that moment just wouldn't
> have had the impact that was necessary to set the tone of the film going

forward. So that was a technique that I started using wherever there were explosions that really needed some depth from the bottom end to resonate.

Just as Chapter 4 showed *Minding the Gap* raising and lowering the volume of sounds coming from the protagonist operating the camera depending on the narrative needs of the scene, *For Sama* does the same. There are many scenes that focus on the drama in front of the camera that have nothing to do with Al-Kateab, and for these scenes the camera mic noise goes unheard. But if she is the focus of the scene, the audience will often hear her breathing and the mic jostling around in order to draw attention to her presence. (*There's someone holding this camera*, the film seems to be saying.) The manipulation of sound is still a fundamental part of the process, it just takes a different form.

In conclusion, each film sets its own parameters for the "reality" of the situation and uses the tools within those parameters to render out a sonic emotional arc for the film. Sound is yet another tool that documentary filmmakers use to deliver a specific and subjective experience.

Notes

1. Mark Kerins, *Beyond Dolby (Stereo): Cinema in the Digital Sound Age* (Bloomington: Indiana University Press, 2010), 53.
2. *Minding the Gap*, directed by Bing Liu (ITVS/Kartemquin Films, 2018), 1:13:30.
3. Mark Kerins, *Beyond Dolby (Stereo)*, 86.
4. This shift in editing practices likely has multiple causes and cannot be solely attributed to the greater fidelity of the soundtrack. However, Doane makes an excellent point about the importance that sound now plays in establishing geography in film scenes.
5. *The Cave*, directed by Feras Fayyad (National Geographic Films, 2019), 00:04:30.

10
Music

> Music is an interpretation. It's the filmmaker who says, "All right, I'm going to make you listen to music here on top of these images to create a certain impression." It's impressionism. I don't think documentary is a form of impressionism. It's realism, and music has no place there.
>
> —Michel Brault

Brault, cinematographer of the landmark film *Chronicle of a Summer*, expressed a sentiment shared by many in the cinema verité movement when he made this statement. In that era of the 1960s and 1970s the use of music in documentaries was viewed with suspicion. "Music envelops, puts us to sleep, helps bad cuts pass unnoticed, and gives an artificial rhythm to pictures that don't have, and never will have, any rhythm of their own," stated Jean Rouch in 1963. "In short," he concluded, "music is the opium of the cinema." The rejection of music in documentaries came about as part of a larger movement that had great distrust for the sentimentality, exaggerated emotionality, and slavery to convention that pervaded many Hollywood studio productions in the middle of the twentieth century, as well as how music was used to accentuate all those trends. Directors such as Michelangelo Antonioni ("Hollywood is like being nowhere and talking to nobody about nothing"), Ingmar Bergman, Luis Buñuel, Alain Resnais, Claude Chabrol, and Carlos Saura fashioned films that used music sparingly or employed it in unconventional ways, and documentary filmmakers like Frederick Wiseman, the Maysles brothers, Shirley Clarke, and Jean Rouch removed it entirely from their films. If music is a shortcut to revealing the subtext of a scene,

How Documentaries Work. Jacob Bricca, Oxford University Press. © Oxford University Press 2023.
DOI: 10.1093/oso/9780197554104.003.0011

these directors were more apt to want to let the subtext be *discovered* rather than made explicit.

Yet as of this writing, music is in great abundance in all corners of the documentary and nonfiction world. The vast majority of documentary films and television shows have a music track, and documentary composers are in high demand. Indeed, composer Nainita Desai's experience with a particular director shows just how far the pendulum has swung.

> Early in my career I was hired to work with this legendary documentary filmmaker in the UK. And when I went into the spotting session with him the first thing he said to me was, "I have to tell you that I don't like music in films." Now, ten films and twenty years later, when we work together, he says to me, "Here's the film, do what you want."

Fear of Music

To explore the contemporary use of music in documentaries, we need to first explore the intellectual foundation of this distrust of music, for its influence lives on in how composers think about writing music for documentaries and how it is produced and mixed.

The verité purists argued that the world of Hollywood films was one in which music—an element *external* to the world of the characters—intrudes upon them at will. It blares, *"How romantic!"* *"What a funny moment!"* *"The tension mounts . . ."* and *"Gotcha! Surprise!"* over them, narrating their experience and making them mere marionettes of the filmmaker; it overtly manipulates the audience into feeling a particular emotion that is inauthentic to the images themselves. To use music in this way in a documentary, the argument goes, would be to imply that the same relationship holds: the people in the story are just creatures of the storyteller, overtly arranged for a particular purpose and containing no autonomy of their own. Audience members, by extension, are equally disrespected since their emotions are being toyed with in a crass way. If music, as Claudia Gorbman describes, "throws a net around the floating visual signifier" and "pins down the meaning of the visuals [just as] adjectives and adverbs pin down the meaning of the nouns and verbs they are attached to,"[1] then music holds no justifiable place in any documentary with pretensions of a credible relationship to the truth.[2]

This argument has manifest merits. Looking at the history of film music, one finds evidence for just such bald manipulative intentions. As Katherine Kalinak has noted, the earliest musical encyclopedias, which were inventories of sheet music, were created for precisely this purpose (see Figure 10.1). They contained such items as "Hurry Music" (for struggles, duel, mob and fire scenes) and "Indian Music" (an all-purpose cue for Native Americans onscreen). The cues relied heavily on cliché to fix meaning, using "tremolo for suspense, pizzicato for sneakiness, and dissonance for villainy."[3] Thus, this argument successfully identifies music's common role as a cue for Pavlovian emotional responses from the audience.

Yet this perspective is arguably somewhat naive, for several more wrinkles of complexity must be folded into the discussion. First, to decry "manipulation" in music without acknowledging the strongly manipulative role played by the picture and sound editing in sculpting the very scenes that music is meant to support is to play favorites with some parts of the documentary process at the expense of others. Second, the antimusic argument may also carry with it an insupportably ascetic view of documentary practice. It assumes that music must, by definition, introduce falseness and manipulation. Yet this assumption can be challenged: Can music not bring an audience emotionally *closer* to the truth of the participants' experience rather than driving them away? Might the audience not see *deeper* into the psychology of the participants by letting music shade the emotions in a particular way that brings out a nuance that might not have been visible before? Can the audience not get closer to human experience *through* (rather than despite) documentary's more performative impulses? When Werner Herzog claimed his allegiance to the

SAM FOX
MOVING PICTURE
MUSIC

By J. S. ZAMECNIK

VOL. I PRICE 50 CENTS

CONTENTS

	Page
Festival March	2
Indian Music	3
Oriental Veil Dance	4
Chinese Music	5
Oriental Music	6
Mexican or Spanish Music	8
Funeral March	9
Death Scene	9
Church Music	10
War Scene	
Part 1 (In Military Camp)	11
Part 2 (Off to the Battle)	12
Part 3 (The Battle)	12 and 13
Cowboy Music	14
Grotesque or Clown Music	15
Mysterioso-Burglar Music	16
Mysterioso-Burglar Music	16
Hurry Music (for struggles)	17
Hurry Music (for duels)	17
Hurry Music	18
Hurry Music (for mob or fire scenes)	19
Storm Scene	20
Sailor Music	21
Fairy Music	21
Plaintive Music	22
Plaintive Music	23

Copyright MCMXIII by Sam Fox Publishing Co., Cleveland, Ohio. (International Copyright Secured)

Published by Sam Fox Pub. Co. *Cleveland, O.*

Figure 10.1 The Sam Fox Moving Picture Music catalog, with sheet music for every type of scene (1913)

"ecstatic truth" of a documentary, perhaps this is what he meant, for the moments of great human feeling generated by a film are themselves arguably a vital form of truth.[4] By a priori marking the performative and interpretational aspects of music as illegitimate, this perspective risks ignoring the highly complex meanings created by music in documentaries.

Consider the use of music in the 2021 Academy Award nominee *Time*, which chronicles the journey of Fox Rich, a woman who worked for twenty years to free her husband from prison while bringing up their five children on her own. "On June 15, 1999, my husband was sentenced to sixty years in prison without the benefit of probation, parole, or suspension of sentence," states Rich as the audience sees a close-up of the life-sized cardboard cutout of her husband that she keeps in her home. "Sixty years of human life!" she exclaims, letting the enormity of the number sink in. Her mother picks up the thread in an interview, marveling at the pain and injustice of the situation as she says, "It's almost like slavery time when the white man keeps you there until he figures it's time for you to get out." Emotions of frustration, sadness, and anger are clearly justified as a part of this family's long journey. But the musical cue that plays underneath, a transcendent solo piano piece by Emahoy Tsegueé-Maryam Guébrou recorded in 1967, injects a huge dose of hope and resolve into the mix. With the joy and weightlessness of the music countering the heaviness of the situation, it becomes clear to the audience that Rich's experience is multilayered and complex: she is beaten down *and* sturdy, sad *and* resolute, outraged *and* calm. The music in this film helps to build a vastly more nuanced experience for the audience.

It is also worth considering music's role as a catalyst for catharsis. If the ascetic perspective sees music as tainting the cinematic experience with artificiality because of its overt emotional content, an alternate perspective might see that same emotional content as a welcome invitation for the audience to engage with hearts as well as minds. If the images are left unaccompanied, the argument goes, this leaves them unexamined and inert—the "accountant's truth," as Herzog would have it. Music transforms the images by realizing their emotional meaning. If the scenes in a documentary display moments of great pain or joy, music is the act of the film itself *acknowledging* that pain or joy and becoming a vessel of human feeling. It is as if the music were produced by the images and has earned a place at the table along with the other elements. Indeed, many documentary composers see themselves in precisely this light. "I think of myself not so much as a composer, but more as someone with a music specialization who is part of the storytelling team," says composer Mark Adler.

The push and pull between these perspectives is alive today in the considerations made behind the scenes by documentary composers. "The main difference between a narrative and a doc is that in a narrative there are actors working off of a script portraying someone other than themselves, whereas in a doc, there are real people being themselves opening up their lives onscreen," says composer Jonathan Zalben (*Axios*, *On Pointe*).

> For me, these two scenarios can require a different approach and a different sensitivity when it comes to score. While both actors and real people are coming from a place of sensitivity and vulnerability, when you are dealing with real people's lives, the music needs to be a bit more careful to support the people and the scene.

Composer Miriam Cutler (*RBG*, *The Hunting Ground*) agrees.

> If I'm scoring a Superman movie there is a villain and a hero, and I can go all the way with my music because the point of the film is the heightened stakes and the drama, and there's not supposed to be a great deal of nuance. Documentaries, on the other hand, are often trying to show us shades of gray and deliver the content in a deeply exploratory way that helps bring illumination, rather than just drama.

These quotations are representative of how documentary directors and composers think of the role of music in contemporary nonfiction films and television shows. There is widespread enthusiasm for the use of music, but also a feeling that it can intersect counterproductively with the realist premise if used carelessly. "Give me a shot of a girl crying, and I can either make her look like she lost her father, or that she didn't get a lollipop, depending on the music," says composer Miriam Cutler, "but I would rather not be asked to make the music do such heavy lifting."

Film versus Television

How does the use of music vary across the full spectrum of nonfiction films and television shows? On one end of the spectrum, we find "art house" documentary films. These films get a substantial part of their legitimation from film festivals, the art world, and academia, which tend to reward more avant-garde tendencies. They are often funded, at least in part, by grants and donations, and are not as directly tied to commercial imperatives. In these realms it is generally accepted as a positive to put the audience on a longer leash, letting meanings float a little more freely and letting viewers "make up their own mind." The infrequent use of music in the 2016 documentary film *Cameraperson* is instructive. A highly personal meditation on the act of filming by noted nonfiction cinematographer Kirsten Johnson, the film has no music cues for the first thirty-one minutes of its running time. When a highly romantic and expressive piece of orchestral music is introduced at full volume during one of the film's only montages, it turns its images of a family living life in rural Bosnia into a section that feels instantly cinematic.[5] Because of the film's subject matter and because the cue is so anomalous with the rest of the film, the section also plays as *self-consciously cinematic*, calling attention to the role that the music is playing in creating the emotions in the first place. Watching this section of *Cameraperson* is to simultaneously feel the sweeping emotion of the moment and to *notice the feeling* of being swept up by a music cue in a documentary film.

At the other end of the spectrum we find reality TV, in which the use of music is both ubiquitous (pinning down emotional content in nearly every scene) and shameless (accentuating drama and suspense in ways that relentlessly push extreme emotions rather than subtle ones). A 2003 episode of the short-lived show *Married by America* is a good example: the music is designed for instant legibility as well as performative drama. During a single seventy-five-second scene, the audience witnesses Stephen and Billie Jeanne's relationship go from giddy premarital bliss (discussion of wedding vows) to a fight that threatens their entire relationship ("dumb jerk," she says after he won't come clean about how he'd like the chicken prepared for dinner.) The music at the beginning is all lilting, romantic strings strongly evoking "Here Comes the Bride," but by the end it has moved to dark, foreboding synth tones.

As composer Ted Reichman puts it,

> In projects that are designed for television, the tendency is to do wall-to-wall music; there is simply the expectation that there will be music all the time. I think it is almost like a reflex. This doesn't mean it is good or bad, I think it is just a part of the cinematic television landscape now and has been that way for a long time.

This means that everything that appears on Discovery, TLC, Bravo, HGTV, and other cable channels offering unscripted programming shares this characteristic. Interestingly, it is also shared by nearly all docuseries on Netflix.[6] Composer Nainita Desai's recent experience working on a Netflix docuseries is instructive here.

> The director wanted lots of space and atmosphere, much more than you usually see in those documentaries, and I thought, "Okay, well, let's go with it." And then Netflix watched it and said, "We want it to be more propulsive, we want there to be more tension," even though it was totally at odds with what the director's brief was. We had to find a compromise, so I built in more cues that had tension and propulsion and energy.

Verité versus Expository, Interviews versus Archival

The use of music in documentaries also varies greatly by which documentary elements are dominant in the film at any given time. Here the realist premise of the documentary project comes into play yet again. A verité scene, which is coded more strongly as "realist" and is meant to convey emotion with the purity of its approach, is less likely to have music supporting it than a montage or a scene dominated by archival or reenactment. As composer Nathan Halpern notes,

> In the docs I've scored that were done in a cinema verité style, like *Rich Hill* or *Minding the Gap*, the rule of thumb is to stay out of the naturalist dialogue scenes. They're for real. And the moments where you're coming in musically are the more subjective moments or moments of montage. Not that you're never scoring those verité scenes, but you're more selective about it. Whereas in the films that use a lot of archival and talking heads, you're more likely going to have music running consistently to tie things together and to bring that more relentless presence.[7]

And documentarian Steve James follows a similar rule.

> I have my own personal rule to *not* score strong verité scenes in my films. I want the power of the moment captured to carry the emotion more purely, without imposing this layer of added emotion, or importance, or editorializing.

The volume level at which music is played is another variable. In general, music must play second fiddle to dialogue, whose legibility is paramount. "If you think about how sound is arranged in a theater," notes Jonathan Zalben, "there's a dedicated channel in the center just for the voice—there are no other elements that get to be in the center. It literally takes center stage. And that really shows the importance of the spoken word in any kind of filmmaking, including documentary."

While music will generally avoid competing with voice, it still matters *what is on the screen* when the voice is heard. If the interviewee appears onscreen, it is generally less likely that music will be high in the mix, whereas if other material takes up the visual field (archival images, reenactment, animation), this leaves the composer more room to intervene. As Ted Reichman relates,

I did a film that was essentially a horror story. It was a very violent story about the end of World War II with refugees and battleships and the like. But most of the footage onscreen consisted of interviews. So it felt a little bit bizarre to be scoring a really dramatic battle—which is what they wanted—over this image of this very frail woman with a weak voice. It was hard for me because you are looking and hearing something that is very different from the story that she is telling. It is a very grandiose story, but the cinematic content isn't there to support the idea of a grandiose musical gesture.

Tone

Music's function goes beyond the moment-to-moment work of bringing out emotional and thematic colors in specific scenes. Crucially, it is also building a unified tone for the entire work. It is yet another way that a filmmaker has of imposing coherence on what can otherwise be a sprawling and incoherent collection of experience fragments, and documentary composers are keenly aware of this necessity. As Miriam Cutler states,

As a composer you must have a unified vision for the film. I can't suddenly go from a string quartet and then turn it into a bluegrass band in the next scene unless you want people to go, *What's that?* I ask myself, "How do I unify? How do I make a cohesive musical narrative that goes with the narrative of the film?" It's kind of like if you're having a burger and fries, and all of a sudden, they bring spaghetti and Thai food—it would make some people sick.

Thus, music is crucial in its role of telling the audience something about the overall framework and approach of the film.

As the first notes of the score for the 2014 Robert Kenner film *Merchants of Doubt* play, one can immediately sense what is in store. The visuals show a magician putting the final touches on his costume and practicing a couple of quick moves with a deck of cards, while soft vibraphone notes put the audience in the world of a

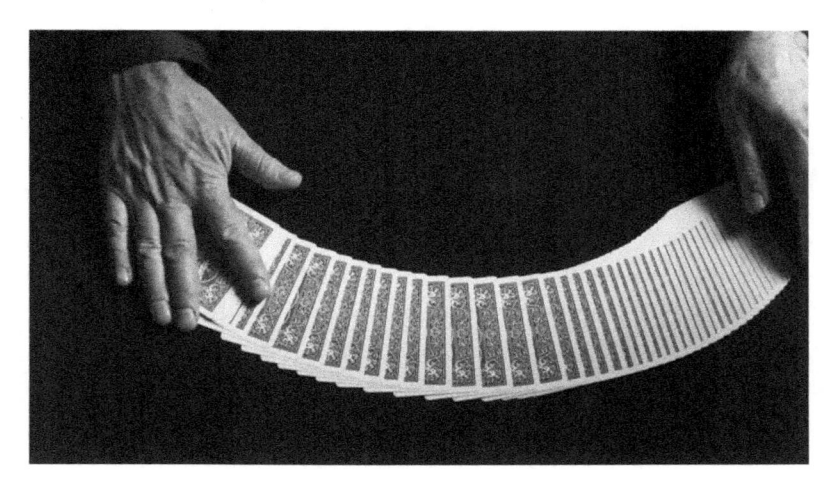

Figure 10.2 A magician prepares his cards in *Merchants of Doubt*

pleasant, dreamy fantasy (see Figure 10.2). As the music continues, the audience hears a hint of mystery from the plucking in the string section, but there is also darkness and sense of foreboding brought in by the minor key of the strings, as well as a hint of a sense of humor from the quick changes in tempo. As its composer Mark Adler recalls,

> Robbie Kenner hired me to work on *Merchants of Doubt* before they even started shooting, and we were exploring the tone of the film and the score. We had been trying out different musical references with limited success, when one day he said to me, "It's a comedy about the end of the world." And I immediately wrote that down on a little Post-it and stuck it up on my computer display. This one little phrase was more valuable than hours of other discussions about possible instrumentation and tempo might have been. That's something I could really work with as a composer.

As the film plays out, its dark humor becomes apparent when life-and-death issues of public health are treated cavalierly by the captains of industry whose bottom lines would be adversely affected by the revelation of inconvenient truths. The magician in the opening scene is a metaphor for the sleight of hand practiced by the PR machines in the belly of the corporate beast.

The music composed for the HBO newsmagazine show *Axios* is also instructive. Before the show ever existed, *Axios* was purely an online news outlet. News from *Axios* was quite different from any other news provider, though: it presented the news as bullet points rather than in the typical pyramid structure of paragraphs and "stories." It was composer Jonathan Zalben's job to turn this style into actual music.

> They explained to me what *Axios* was, and the phrase they used was "smart brevity." That was the branding. And so every aspect of what they wanted to do was to encapsulate that idea of smart brevity with a clean aesthetic and something that wasn't your usual fare in journalism. So when I got down to work, I knew that the big-horn thing that you're used to hearing on the nightly news was not going to be the direction. Instead, while there are some strings which are pretty traditional, there is also a lot of percussion and a lot of synth elements as well. So, it's got an organic and electric feel, and it gives it a fresh kind of sound, but still familiar in a way.

Procedural Music

Another function of music, less overtly emotional but equally as powerful, is to subtly buttress the forward narrative momentum of the film. Place music under any interstitial moment in a documentary (a montage, a few moments between scenes) and it instantly seems to come to life, reassuring the audience that they are in good hands and that the plot is indeed thickening.

As Jonathan Zalben says,

> I guess you could call this procedural music—it's music that says a task is happening or information is being conveyed. It almost serves a timekeeping function, giving you a bit of forward momentum. It's a very contemporary kind of writing. It's not particularly emotional.

There's nothing heavy happening, but without it you might feel adrift.

Another name for this might be "forward motion music." Interestingly, it refers more to the machinery of the storytelling than it does to the emotions of a particular scene or the development of any individual character. It would be inaccurate to say that it's without emotional content—for it would be impossible to create music *without* emotional content—but those emotional shadings are *on top of* its other function, which is a sort of self-admiration for the process of storytelling itself. *The plot is turning, the story's getting good, we all really want to know how this is going to end!* it purrs.

The music cues chosen for the National Geographic series *City So Real*, about the history-making 2018 Chicago mayoral election, offer an excellent example. Made up of music composed by Chicago musicians from across many decades, the cues seem uniquely rooted in the city that is the subject of the show. The cue for the close of Episode 2 ("You've Changed" by the Ramsey Lewis Trio) is a relaxed and warm ballad, all tasteful piano runs and expansive bass backing, and brings a soulfulness and solidity to the shots of the city after the audience has witnessed a bruising and at times corrupt mayoral primary, as if it say, *This place with so many problems is also deeply human; it lives and breathes just like the individuals who make it up.* The musical cue over the moment in the concluding episode when Chicago reckons with violent protests over the murder of George Floyd ("Quartz" by Makaya McCraven) is a tense percussion solo whose tinny stick-on-metal sound feels like a rickety machine on the verge of collapse, as if to say, *This is the part of the story where city may just explode,* before it settles into a more consistent rhythm and shifts gears to pose the question, *What will be the next chapter? Will the churn and grind of politics manage to turn this into a tale of positive systemic change?*[8] In each of these cases, the music seems to be speaking to the give and take of the storytelling apparatus as much as it is speaking to the emotions of the moment. Its placement at moments that occur between other scenes is part of what gives it its significance.

A closely related kind of documentary music is exemplified by the work of Philip Glass, whose minimalist works have become a genre unto themselves. (His IMDB page lists an astonishing 164 credits as composer.) Since he first agreed to the pleadings of director Godfrey Reggio to score the 1983 film *Koyaanisqatsi* and in countless other films since, Glass's music does not tend to vary greatly in its emotional tone over the course of a film, declining to reinforce or contradict the emotional shadings of scenes in the sculpted way that music often does (punching in when dialogue is absent, filling in the contours created by the editing). Instead of providing targeted commentary, it provides context, building another layer of atmosphere that seems to pervade everything. "It is providing a sort of backdrop," says composer Ted Reichman. "It's like invisible scenery that creates a space for the viewer to think about what they are seeing and hearing."

* * *

We have barely scratched the surface of music's complex and varied relationship to images in documentary. Indeed, it is precisely the ineffable feeling that can seem to emanate from the images that is so sought-after by documentary filmmakers looking to find another dimension in their work via a sophisticated score. One thing is certain: it is a central, defining force in the audience's experience.

Notes

1. Katherine Kalinak, *Film Music: A Very Short Introduction* (Oxford: Oxford University Press, 2020), 18.
2. Another reason why audiences may reject the use of music is if the subtext doesn't feel authentic. As composer Nathan Halpern says, "When we're creating music, we are sort of dialing into and dialing up a subtext. And if that subtext is inauthentic and feels like it's being imposed, then unconsciously, the audience will rebel. On some level, they can feel that this is the hand of the composer and the hand of the director coming on a bit too strong. It's like someone's flicking your ear while you're watching the movie."
3. Kalinak, *Film Music*, 44.

4. Herzog coined this phrase on April 3, 1999, when he made his "Minnesota Declaration" at the Walker Art Center in Minneapolis. Point 5 declared, "There are deeper strata of truth in cinema, and there is such a thing as poetic, ecstatic truth. It is mysterious and elusive, and can be reached only through fabrication and imagination and stylization." Roger Ebert, "Herzog's Minnesota Declaration: Defining 'Ecstatic Truth,'" *RogerEbert.com*, April 30, 1999, https://www.rogerebert.com/roger-ebert/herzogs-minnesota-declaration-defining-ecstatic-truth.

5. *Cameraperson*, directed by Kirsten Johnson (Big Mouth Productions / Fork Films, 2016), 00:32:16.

6. Netflix's subscription model theoretically makes it less susceptible to the pressures of having to deliver audiences to advertisers, which has been theorized as a reason for the more blunt aesthetics of broadcast television. However, much of Netflix's programming and interface (instantly hurrying the audience to the next episode via the aggressive autoplay feature, for instance) is designed with a similar goal of keeping the viewer from leaving its orbit.

7. "Composers' Roundtable: Narrative vs. Documentary," May 12, 2021 (online members-only forum). Used by permission from Halpern and the Society of Composers and Lyricists.

8. *City So Real*, Episode 5, directed by Steve James (National Geographic Films, 2020), 00:16:10–00:17:43.

Conclusion

The Brave New World of Hybridity in Documentary

It is my sincere hope that the preceding chapters of this book have helped to illuminate some of the mysteries about how documentaries work. But I have some bad news: much of what I have said is about to be wrong. Film language, like any other language, is not a fixed system—it evolves with the times. As much as we might try, coming up with a definitive guide to the rules of documentary film language is doomed to eventual failure because the language itself is a moving target.

To posit an analogy, consider the humble exclamation point. Anecdotal evidence suggests that its use in work-related emails (*Thank you! Wonderful! Perfect!*) was relatively rare two decades ago but has since become much more commonplace. As the frequency of its use has increased, its power to convey genuine excitement has waned. Whereas the exclamation point used to deliver the suggestion of genuine excitement, it's now been downgraded to a healthy dose of chipper friendliness. To get the same effect, "You and I might be using *two* exclamation points in another twenty years," said linguist John McWhorter in a recent interview.[1]

Consider for a moment just how much film language has changed in the relatively short period of its existence. Up through the 1950s it was unheard of for Hollywood fiction films to stray from a tight set of conventions for the progression of shots in a scene. A wide shot had to come first, and a medium shot had to come before a close-up as scenes invariably moved from wide to close. That rule was challenged by the jump cuts and the innovative approaches to narrative

How Documentaries Work. Jacob Bricca, Oxford University Press. © Oxford University Press 2023.
DOI: 10.1093/oso/9780197554104.003.0012

of the French New Wave and has long since been abandoned; it is arguably more common today to find scenes starting with a detail shot or a close-up, only later revealing the master shot.

Likewise, documentary film language has grown and evolved over the years as it has progressed through many stylistic revolutions and counterrevolutions. With each new generation, the churn of stylistic signals has become more intense. As the form continues to evolve in the instant streaming environment of the digital age, it is no wonder that filmmakers have adopted an increasingly fluid and eclectic range of approaches to the documentary filmmaking enterprise. Films that once might have had a strict presence framing now mix and match between them; films that might have prosecuted their stories with a limited number of elements now dabble in the full array of them. In sum, the conventions that this book has taken pains to describe are in flux.

An example of a documentary convention that has undergone a rapid evolution in meaning is the direct-to-camera interview, in which the interviewee looks squarely into the lens. Its use has exploded lately, and it is fast becoming the dominant mode of interview address in docuseries. Whereas it was once a highly charged statement to have the subject look into the camera, full of bracing intimacy, it's now just one option among others, not much different from the choice to have them look offscreen at the interviewer. Audiences have become used to people looking directly at them via the first-person video diaries on reality television, the vlogs and how-to videos on YouTube, and the ubiquitous selfie, such that the intense testimonial/confessional aura it once carried (think Errol Morris circa *The Thin Blue Line*) has diminished. Shows will now regularly feature these kinds of interviews even when the slant of the show is more "lightweight investigative documentary" (such as *Bad Boy Billionaires: India*; see Figure C.1) than "intimate/confessional portrait." Its ubiquity has diffused its meaning.

Another example is the increasing prevalence of visual references to the act of filming. A traditional documentary interview shows no trace of production equipment in the shot. But it is now commonplace to reference the act of filming the interview in some way,

Figure C.1 A direct-to-camera interview in *Bad Boy Billionaires: India*

whether by including film production gear (lights, C-stands) in the periphery of the shot or having the subject make some sort of reference to the filming. (An increasingly common trope, as seen in Morgan Neville's *Roadrunner: A Film about Anthony Bourdain* and Mariem Pérez Riera's *Rita Moreno: Just a Girl Who Decided to Go for It*, is to show the subjects walking onto the set and taking their place in the interview chair near the start of the film, as if to say, *Here we go! Let the story commence.*) In *Controlling Britney Spears*, an FX documentary presented by the *New York Times*, interview subjects often appear not only in their own interview shots but also on field monitors on the set (see Figure C.2).

What meaning should audiences take from this? One could justify its use in *Controlling Britney Spears* as consistent with the subject matter (a look at a highly public celebrity whose life has been lived in the media eye), but maybe it just looks cool. An increasingly casual orientation toward using such footage now seems to pertain, at least in more commercial documentaries.

A third trend is the increasingly subtle—and sometimes nonexistent—cues employed to mark the use of reenactments in documentary. Take an opening scene from the Netflix documentary *Bikram: Yogi, Guru, Predator*, which explores the astonishing worldwide success of Bikram Yoga and the disturbing accounts of sexual assault and psychological manipulation by its namesake

Figure C.2 An interview in *Controlling Britney Spears*

Bikram Choudhury. As the audience hears an audio recording of Bikram beginning one of his classes they see a hand enter the frame to turn an indoor thermostat all the way up. Sweaty bodies perform their poses in extremely shallow focus shots that perfectly frame the participants with smooth, professional camera moves (Figure C.3).

Finally, an archival still image arrives on the screen of Choudhury leading a class from back in the day, surrounded by a sea of followers (Figure C.4). Up to this point in the scene, *everything* has been a reenactment, though there are no obvious visual treatments to mark them as such. The coding is so subtle that it is simply left up to the deductive reasoning of the audience to discern what must be going on. It is the very professionalism of the camera work and its au courant shallow focus style that provides the tip-off. *This couldn't have been shot back in 1988 because it looks too good,* one muses. *The voice recording must be archival and the rest of it must be reenactment.*

In this case, it is still possible for an audience member to spot the reenactment. But the burying of reenactment deep inside the fabric of documentary—with no distinguishing characteristics whatsoever—is proceeding apace. It was recently revealed that the

Figure C.3 A reenactment scene from *Bikram: Yogi, Guru, Predator*

Figure C.4 An archival still from *Bikram: Yogi, Guru, Predator*

mural of a smiling Anthony Bourdain that is playfully defaced by his friend David Choe at the end of *Roadrunner* as a statement against Bourdain's posthumous deification ("Anthony would fucking hate [it]") was painted by the production in order to be defaced in the first place. Thus, what seemed on first glance to be verité was actually staged for the camera.

This is part of a blurring of boundaries between fiction and non-fiction that is occurring in many corners of the documentary world. In recent years, at least one or two films make it into the documentary category at Sundance that tug aggressively at the boundaries of the form. *Bloody Nose, Empty Pockets*, a 2020 entry ostensibly about the closing night in a Las Vegas dive bar called The Roaring 20s, was actually filmed in Terrytown, Louisiana, and featured barflies from a host of nearby watering holes who were invited to play out the fictional closing of the joint. The official Sundance festival materials for the US Documentary Competition describe the film thusly, coyly dropping hints about the hybridity of the production while refusing to clarify the details:

> In the shadows of the bright lights of Las Vegas, it's last call for a beloved dive bar known as the Roaring 20s. Its regulars, a cross section of American life, form a community—tight-knit yet forged in happenstance, teetering between dignity and debauchery, reckoning with the past as they face an uncertain future. That's the premise, at least; the reality is as unreal as the world they're escaping from....
>
> [The filmmakers'] beguiling approach to nonfiction storytelling makes for a foggy memory of experience lost in empty shot glasses and puffs of smoke.

This blurry state of affairs across the doc landscape seems clearly related to the recent explosion of content across a wide variety of platforms, where a film made in one institutional setting will play right alongside another with no differentiation or distinction. (Watching *Bloody Nose, Empty Pockets* at Sundance is a very different experience from clicking on it absentmindedly on a streamer, for instance, where the cues about its hybridity can easily be lost and there is no sense of a larger conversation taking place about its meaning.) Again, we have come full circle to the fact that much of the potential confusion about documentaries comes from the different spaces occupied by filmmakers and their audiences. It's important to note that with both *Roadrunner* and *Bloody Nose, Empty Pockets*, the filmmakers were happy to discuss the details of the actual filming process when asked about it by the press and were eager to engage in a conversation about it with their audiences. But is that enough? What, if anything, do they owe their audiences?

One thing is certain: to fully understand what they see, audiences must become more active in their evaluation of documentaries and should consider extrafilmic assets and information (marketing materials, press, the reputation of the production company) as a vital part of the film experience. For instance, PBS takes its duties as a public broadcaster seriously and does rigorous fact-checking on any claims made in films released under its *Frontline, Independent Lens*, and *POV* umbrellas, and does not allow any supplementary funding for these projects to come from entities with a political stake in the issues at hand. There is an entirely different set of rules for films released by other outfits, where funding may come from the very persons depicted onscreen, a fact only revealed by a careful look at the end credits.

Audiences should also be aware of the effects of the increasing commercialization and commodification of the form. Most docuseries being produced today, for instance, are created as pieces of entertainment, rather than as objects of art, pieces of rigorous journalism, or instruments of pedagogical instruction. Though there are important exceptions, in general they tend to value instant audience pleasure (via humor, relentless narrative propulsion, and visual eye candy) over more subtle qualities such as formal rigor and psychological complexity. Feature-length documentaries purchased and produced by Netflix, Hulu, and other streamers are also trending in this direction, which is unsurprising when one considers the motivations that drive their acquisitions. "There are two general categories of content that streamers are looking for," said Endeavor Content senior VP of documentary Kevin Iwashina in a recent interview in *Variety*. "Docs for subscriber acquisition, and for subscriber retention."[2] If every documentary needs either a big-name subject or director (to attract subscribers) or a style that aids easy consumption (to retain them), then such trends are almost a foregone conclusion. Stated another way, if the primary job of the documentary is entertainment, then the thoughtfulness of its delivery is less important than the density of its experience, and many documentaries today have more in common stylistically with advertising than with any other discernible film genre.

Film critic and scholar Dana Stevens seemed to hit the nail on the head in her *Slate Culture Gabfest* review of Amazon's *LuLaRich*, a docuseries about a multi-level marketing juggernaut gone bad.

> I'm tired of this format of documentary. It's this . . . slick, cutesy style . . . with the constant ominous plinky music in the background. [There are] very short cuts of interviews, . . . social media posts being montaged quickly onto the screen. . . . you never spend too long with any one person. [It's] that whole style of sensory bombardment.

We can name some more characteristics of this ascendant style of documentary filmmaking: ubiquitous drone shots that glide in frictionless surveillance of the landscape, b-roll shots taken from moving cameras, playful and ironic bursts of archival material used for comedic effect. These are often incorporated not in the hopes of generating a coherent message or revealing anything profound about the human condition, but rather in making the product able to compete in the attention economy of our day.

That style is ascendant, but far from ubiquitous. For every film with a jumble of references and approaches there is another that treats the relationship between the subject(s), the camera, and the filmmaker in a formally rigorous way. Take *Tell Me Who I Am*, the documentary about two brothers split apart by a terrible secret. They are each seen walking onto the studio set for their own interviews at the start of the film. As the film continues, they are only ever seen in *individual* interview shots. This is contrasted with the climactic conclusion when they share the same frame for the first time and achieve reconciliation after walking *together* onto the set for their final interview. In this case, the form has been purposefully tied to the content and used to deliver a highly specific meaning. Ditto with the rigorously constrained approach of the recent all-archival documentaries *Mike Wallace Is Here* and *Fire of Love*, neither of which need a single contemporary interview or reenactment to deliver their highly original portraits. (*Mike Wallace Is Here* doesn't even use narration.) And the number of documentaries making bold, powerful artistic statements with equally profound political messages has not dissipated. One could point to the intricate interweaving of archival footage with verité scenes in Garrett Bradley's masterful *Time*, which makes its urgent antiracist plea in bracing black-and-white as a way of elegantly dissolving the boundaries between past and present; or to the utter joyfulness of Libby Dina Cohn and J. P. Sniadecki's *People's Park*, which turns the act of people-watching in a Chinese park into a fine art by forcing the viewer into a position of patient observation by filming the action in a single take.

All of which is to say that despite the extreme hybridity and lack of restraint of our current moment—or perhaps because of it—documentary analysis is still vitally important. Every image and sound in a documentary comes from somewhere. What is the provenance of those images and sounds? What are their formal characteristics? What is the logic of their arrangement? What kind of presence of the filmmaker is implied—or pointedly ignored? These questions are all urgently worth posing. Finally, as you sit and let the last moments of a documentary wash over you, it's worth interrogating your own experience and asking, "What did I really see?"

Notes

1. EconTalk podcast with John McWhorter, August 21, 2017, https://www.econt alk.org/john-mcwhorter-on-the-evolution-of-language-and-words-on-the-move/.
2. Gregg Goldstein, "Nonfiction Producers and Directors Talk How to Make Docs Pop in Crowded Marketplace," *Variety*, October 30, 2021, https://variety.com/ 2021/film/markets-festivals/afm-documentary-1235100214/.

Acknowledgments

This book began as a short presentation about the use of pauses in documentaries at the 2018 conference of the University Film and Video Association. Fortuitously, Oxford University Press humanities editor Norman Hirschy was in the audience and saw something he liked. Ever since he pitched me on the idea for this book, it has been a great pleasure to work with him. I could not ask for a more supportive partner in this endeavor.

This book would not have been possible without the generosity of all of the documentary filmmakers and craftspeople who sat down with me for extended interviews. To Chadi Abo, Mark Adler, Peter Albrechtsen, Miriam Cutler, Jacob Dammas, Nainita Desai, Feras Fayyad, George Foulgham, Steve James, Helen Kearns, Tamara Kotevska, Penny Lane, Bing Liu, Dan Partland, Jason Rosenfield, J. P. Sniadecki, Jez Spencer, Ljubomir Stefanov, Aaron Wickenden, Jonathan Zalben and Amy Ziering: your wisdom, honesty, and experience are woven throughout this book. An additional thanks to Mark S. Andrew, David Michael Maurer, Jim Ruxin, and Karol Urban, who responded to email and survey queries.

As I developed drafts of the manuscript, I sought feedback a handful of readers. Jonathan Crosby, one of my longtime filmmaking partners and one of the best documentary minds around, gave no-nonsense notes that helped me cut through the clutter of my own ideas. Craig Huston, DGA likewise helped bring much greater clarity to my writing; he questioned my excessive use of commas and made me stop hiding behind the ironic use of quotation marks, forcing me to say what I really mean. The wonderful filmmaker David Fenster provided incisive comments and useful suggestions that I never would have come up with on my own. The incomparable Bill Nichols kindly gave great encouragement and pointed out a need to bring greater clarity to the moments when I toggled between speaking about filmmakers' intentions and audience responses. Jack Walsh—another great documentary mind—gave me more wonderful notes than I could have dreamed for, making the book better with each one. To each of you, I give my humble and heartfelt thanks. Your honesty and generosity have helped bring this book into being.

There are many other folks I'd also like to acknowledge who did not give direct comments on the work but have influenced my thinking about documentaries. Fiona Otway, thank you for our long, rambling talks—I always feel like I learn something from you. Likewise, getting to share raves and pans with Keith Fulton and Lou Pepe is a singular pleasure—when I see a new film, I always wonder, "What would Keith and Lou think about this one?" Jonathan Robinson: every so often we get to stretch out for a few hours, and I always wonder why it took so long. And to my dear friend Michael Kowalski, who is so omnivorous when it comes to film: thank you for being so supportive of my career over these many years.

I am also tremendously lucky to share a University of Arizona title with the committed, talented, and brilliant faculty, staff, and leadership at the University of Arizona School of Theatre, Film and Television. I truly could not ask for better. And thank you to the students at our fair school, who never fail to ask terrific questions about documentary and do such outstanding creative documentary work.

Finally, I would like to thank the love of my life—and collaborator of my dreams—Lisa Molomot. I gave you the manuscript for a final pass, knowing that nothing would get past you that wasn't up to snuff, and was not disappointed. But more than that, you have given me a life full of adventure, joy, and laughter. Thank you for being you.

Films and Television Shows Cited

A Current Affair. Fox Television Stations Group, 1986–96.

The Act of Killing. Directed by Joshua Oppenheimer, Anonymous, and Christine Cynn. Final Cut for Real. 2012.

Actress. Directed by Robert Greene. 4th Row Films. 2014.

After Tiller. Directed by Martha Shane and Lana Wilson. Code Red Pictures. 2013.

Aging Out. Directed by Roger Weisberg, Maria Finitzo, and Vanessa Roth. Public Policy Productions. 2004.

America to Me. Directed by Steve James. National Geographic Films. 2018.

American Animals. Directed by Bart Layton. Film4 Productions / Lava Bear Films / Raw. 2018.

American Factory. Directed by Julia Reichert and Steven Bognar. Higher Ground Productions. 2019.

American Style. Directed by Michael Selditch and Dan Partland. Vox Entertainment / Doc Shop Productions. 2019.

Amy. Directed by Asif Kapadia. Film4 / On the Corner Films. 2015.

Another Year (You yi nia). Directed by Shengze Zhu. Burn the Film. 2016.

The Atomic Café. Directed by Kevin Rafferty, Jayne Loader, and Pierce Rafferty. The Archives Project. 1982.

Attica. Directed by Stanley Nelson. Showtime. 2021.

Axios. Series directed by Matthew O'Neill and Perri Peltz. HBO. 2018–.

The Bachelor. Created by Mike Fleiss. ABC. 2002–.

Bad Boy Billionaires: India. Series directed by Dylan Mohan Gray, Johanna Hamilton, and Nick Reed. Netflix. 2020.

The Bad Kids. Directed by Keith Fulton and Louis Pepe. Low Key Pictures. 2016.

The Ballad of Ramblin' Jack. Directed by Aiyana Elliott. Crawford Communications / Journeyman Pictures / Plantain Films / Verisimilitude. 2000.

Be Water. Directed by Bao Nguyen. ESPN. 2020.

Before the Flood. Directed by Fisher Stevens. RatPac Documentary Films / Appian Way / Insurgent Docs / Mandarin Film Productions. 2016.

Beyond Scared Straight. A&E Networks. 2011–15.

Bikram: Yogi, Guru, Predator. Directed by Eva Orner. Pulse Films. 2019.

Bitter Money (Ku Quin). Directed by Wang Bing. House on Fire / Gladys Glover / Chinese Shadows. 2016.

The Bleeding Edge. Directed by Kirby Dick. Chain Camera Pictures / Shark Island Productions. 2018.

Bloody Nose, Empty Pockets. Directed by Bill Ross IV and Turner Ross. Department of Motion Pictures / XTR. 2020.

Blue Vinyl. Directed by Judith Helfand and Daniel B. Gold. Toxic Comedy Pictures. 2002.

BNSF. Directed by James Benning. James Benning. 2013.

Breaking2. Directed by Martin Desmond Roe. Dirty Robber. 2017.

Cameraperson. Directed by Kirsten Johnson. Big Mouth Productions / Fork Films. 2016.

Capitalism: A Love Story. Directed by Michael Moore. Dog Eat Dog Films / Overture Films / Paramount Vantage / The Weinstein Company. 2009.

The Cave. Directed by Feras Fayyad. National Geographic Films. 2019.

The Chair. Directed by Robert Drew. Drew Associates / Time-Life. 1963.

The Chronicle of a Summer. Directed by Jean Rouch and Edgar Morin. Argos Films. 1961.

Citizen K. Directed by Alex Gibney. Jigsaw Productions / Passion Pictures / Storyteller Productions. 2019.

The City. Directed by Ralph Steiner and Willard Van Dyke. American Institute of Planners. 1939.

City So Real. Series directed by Steve James. Kartemquin Films. 2020.

Controlling Britney Spears. Directed by Samantha Stark. Times Documentaries. 2021.

Country Music. Directed by Ken Burns. Florentine Films / WETA. 2019.

Couples Therapy. Edgeline Films / Loveless. 2019–21.

Crude. Directed by Joe Berlinger. Entendre Films / RadicalMedia / Red Envelope Entertainment / Third Eye Motion Picture Company. 2009.

David Crosby: Remember My Name. Directed by A. J. Eaton. Vinyl Films / BMG / PCH Films. 2019.

Derrida. Directed by Kirby Dick and Amy Ziering. Jane Doe Films. 2002.

Diego Maradona. Directed by Asif Kapadia. Film4 / Lorton Entertainment / On the Corner Films. 2019.

The Disciple. Directed by Chaitanya Tamhane. Zoo Entertainment. 2020.

Echo in the Canyon. Directed by Andrew Slater. Greenwich Entertainment. 2018.

The Edge of Democracy. Directed by Petra Costa. Violet Films / Busca Vida Films / Simmering Films. 2019.

El Valley Centro. Directed by James Benning. James Benning. 1999.

The 11th Hour. Directed by Leila Conners and Nadia Conners. Appian Way / Greenhour / Tree Media Group. 2007.

Escape at Dannemora. Directed by Ben Stiller. Phosphene / Red Hour Films. 2018.

Face to Face with Connie Chung. CBS Broadcasting, Inc. 1991.

Fahrenheit 9 / 11. Directed by Michael Moore. Dog Eat Dog Films. 2004.

Fantastic Fungi. Directed by Louie Schwartzberg. Moving Art Studio / Reconsider. 2019.

Fast, Cheap & Out of Control. Directed by Errol Morris. American Playhouse / Errol Morris Films / Fourth Floor Pictures. 1997.

The Fight. Directed by Eli Despres, Josh Kriegman, and Elyse Steinberg. Edgeline Films / Bow and Arrow Entertainment / Drexler Films / FireLine Entertainment / Good Gravy Films / XTR. 2020.

Fire at Sea. Directed by Gianfranco Rosi. Stemal Entertainment / 21 Unofilm / Instituto Luce Cinecittá / Rai Cinema / Arte France Cinéma. 2016.

Fire of Love. Directed by Sara Dosa. National Geographic Films / Neon. 2022.

First Position. Directed by Bess Kargman. First Position Films. 2011.

Flee. Directed by Jonas Poher Rasmussen. Final Cut for Real. 2021.

For Sama. Directed by Waad Al-Kateab and Edward Watts. Channel 4 / Frontline. 2019.

Forget Me Not. Directed by Sun Hee Engelstoft. Final Cut for Real / Minch&Films. 2019.

Forks over Knives. Directed by Lee Fulkerson. Monica Beach Media. 2011.

498 Days. Directed by Rania Elmalky. Rania Elmalky. 2019.

Frontline. Public Broadcasting Service. 1983–.

Gaga: Five Foot Two. Directed by Chris Moukarbel. Live Nation Productions / Mermaid Films II / Permanent Wave. 2017.

God Grew Tired of Us. Directed by Christopher Dillon Quinn and Tommy Walker. National Geographic Films / Silver Nitrate Pictures. 2006.

The Great British Baking Show. Love Productions / BBC. 2010–.

Hail Satan? Directed by Penny Lane. Hard Working Movies. 2019.

Hale County This Morning, This Evening. Directed by RaMell Ross. Louverture Films. 2018.

Hands on a Hard Body: The Documentary. Directed by S. R. Bindler. Idea Entertainment / J.K. Livin Productions / Wessex Entertainment Group. 1997.

Hard Copy. Paramount Domestic Television. 1989–99.

Harlan County U.S.A. Directed by Barbara Kopple. Cabin Creek Films. 1976.

Hell's Kitchen. Granada Entertainment / A. Smith & Co. Productions / Upper Ground Enterprises. 2005–.

High School. Directed by Frederick Wiseman. Zipporah Films. 1968.

Honeyland. Directed by Tamara Kotevska and Ljubomir Stefanov. Apolo Media / Trice Films. 2019.

Hoop Dreams. Directed by Steve James. Kartemquin Films. 1994.

Hope in the Time of AIDS. Directed by Tim Hardy and Pete McCormack. Mindset Media. 2007.

The Hunting Ground. Directed by Kirby Dick. Chain Camera Pictures. 2015.

I Am Not Your Negro. Directed by Raoul Peck. Velvet Films / Artémis Productions / Close Up Films / ARTE / ITVS. 2016.

Icarus. Directed by Bryan Fogel. Alex Productions / Chicago Media Project / Diamond Docs / Impact Partners / Makemake. 2017.

Ice on Fire. Directed by Leila Conners. Appian Way / HBO / Tree Media Group. 2019.

If You Really Knew Me. Arnold Shapiro Productions. 2010.

Independent Lens. Independent Television Service. 1999–.

Indies Under Fire: The Battle for the American Bookstore. Directed by Jacob Bricca. Otis Films. 2006.

The Interrupters. Directed by Steve James. Kartemquin Films. 2011.

Intervention. Created by Sam Mettler and Rob Sharenow. GRB Entertainment. 2005–.

The Inventor: Out for Blood in Silicon Valley. Directed by Alex Gibney. HBO Documentary Films / Jigsaw Productions. 2019.

The Invisible War. Directed by Kirby Dick. Chain Camera Pictures / Rise Films / ITVS / Fork Films / Cuomo Cole Productions / Canal+. 2012.

Jackass Forever. Directed by Jeff Tremaine. Paramount Pictures / MTV Films / Dickhouse Productions. 2022.

James Baldwin: Witness. Directed by Angie Corcetti. Peter Jones Productions. 2003.

Jane. Directed by D. A. Pennebaker. Produced by Drew Associates. 1962.

Jane Fonda in Five Acts. Directed by Susan Lacy. HBO Documentary Films / Pentimento Productions. 2018.

The Jinx: The Life and Deaths of Robert Durst. Directed by Andrew Jarecki. HBO Documentary Films / Hit the Ground Running Productions / Blumhouse Productions. 2015.

Joan Jett: Bad Reputation. Directed by Kevin Kerslake. BMG / Blackheart Films / Inaudible Films / Submarine Entertainment. 2018.

John McEnroe: In the Realm of Perfection. Directed by Julien Faraut. UFO Production. 2018.

The Kingmaker. Directed by Lauren Greenfield. Evergreen Pictures / Showtime Documentary Films. 2019.

Koyaanisqatsi. Directed by Godfrey Reggio. IRE Productions / American Zoetrope. 1982.

Leviathan. Directed by Lucien Castaing-Taylor and Verena Paravel. Arrête ton Cinéma. 2012.

Living with Michael Jackson. Directed by Julie Shaw. Granada Television. 2003.

Los. Directed by James Benning. James Benning. 2001.

Los Angeles Plays Itself. Directed by Thom Anderson. Thom Anderson Productions. 2003.

Lost in La Mancha. Directed by Keith Fulton and Louis Pepe. Quixote Films / Low Key Productions / Eastcroft Productions. 2002.

Love Island (UK). ITV Studios / Lifted Entertainment / Motion Content Group. 2015–.

Love Island (US). ITV Entertainment. 2019–20.

LuLaRich. Series directed by Jenner Furst and Julia Willoughby Nason. Story Force Entertainment / The Cinemart. 2021.

Married by America. Series created by Ted Haimes. Chaos Theory / Rocket Science Laboratories / Twentieth Century Fox. 2003.

The Matrix. Directed by Lana Wachowski and Lilly Wachowski. Warner Bros. / Village Roadshow. 1999.

McMillions. Series directed by James Lee Hernandez and Brian Lazarte. FunMeter / HBO / Unrealistic Ideas. 2020.

Merchants of Doubt. Directed by Robert Kenner. Participant. 2014.

Mike Wallace Is Here. Directed by Avi Belkin. Delrio Films / Passion Pictures / Rock Paper Scissors Entertainment. 2019.

Miles Davis: Birth of the Cool. Directed by Stanley Nelson. Firelight Media / Eagle Rock Films. 2019.

Millhouse. Directed by Emile de Antonio. Turin Film Productions. 1971.

Minding the Gap. Directed by Bing Liu. ITVS / Kartemquin Films. 2018.

Missing in Brooks County. Directed by Lisa Molomot and Jeff Bemiss. Sunlight Factory / ITVS / Fork Films / Engel Entertainment. 2020.

Mooney vs. Fowle. Directed by Claude Fournier, Richard Leacock, and James Lipscomb. Produced by James Lipscomb Inc. 1962.

The Motherhood Archives. Directed by Irene Lusztig. Women Make Movies. 2013.

My Kid Could Paint That. Directed by Amir Bar-Lev. A&E Indie Films / Axis Films International / BBC / Passion Pictures. 2007.

My Octopus Teacher. Directed by Pippa Ehrlich and James Reed. Netflix / Off The Fence / The Sea Change Project. 2020.

My Scientology Movie. Directed by John Dower. BBC Films / Red Box Films. 2015.

Nanook of the North. Directed by Robert Flaherty. Les Fréres Revillon. 1922.

Near Death. Directed by Frederick Wiseman. Zipporah Films. 1989.

The Newlywed Game. Created by E. Roger Muir and Nick Nicholson. ABC / Chuck Barris Productions. 1966–74.

90 Day Fiancé. Sharp Entertainment. 2019–.

Not a Love Story: A Film about Pornography. Directed by Bonnie Sherr Klein. National Film Board of Canada. 1981.

Nuts! Directed by Penny Lane. Gland Power Films / Cartuna. 2016.

On Pointe. Series directed by Larissa Bills. DCTV / Imagine Documentaries. 2020–.

On the Pole. Directed by Robert Drew. Produced by Drew Associates / Time Inc. 1960.

On the Record. Directed by Kirby Dick and Amy Ziering. Artemis Rising / Chain Camera Pictures / Impact Partners / Jane Doe Films / Level Forward / Shark Island Productions. 2020.

The Other Side of the Wind. Directed by Orson Welles. Royal Road Entertainment / Les Films de L'Astrophore / SACI / American Film Conservancy. 2018.

Our Time Machine. Directed by S. Leo Chiang and Yang Sun. Walking Iris Media / Fish + Bear Pictures / Breezy Doc / ITVS. 2019.

Outrage. Directed by Kirby Dick. Chain Camera Pictures. 2009.

Parasite. Directed by Bong Joon Ho. CJ Entertainment / Barunson E&A. 2019.

The Peacekeepers. Directed by Paul Cowan. National Film Board of Canada / 13 Production. 2005.

People's Park. Directed by Libbie Dina Cohn and J. P. Sniadecki. Sensory Ethnography Lab. 2013.

The Plow That Broke the Plains. Directed by Pare Lorentz. U.S. Resettlement Administration. 1936.

Polish Illusions. Directed by Jacob Dammas and Helge Renner. Graniza. 2012.

Pool Kings. Glass Entertainment Group / Pink Sneakers Productions / Juma Entertainment / Pie Town Productions / Leftfield Pictures. 2015–.

Powaqqatsi. Directed by Godfrey Reggio. Golan-Globus Productions / NorthSouth / Santa Fe Institute for Regional Education. 1988.

Precious Knowledge. Directed by Ari Palos. Dos Vatos Productions / ITVS. 2011.

Primary. Directed by Robert Drew. Drew Associates. 1960.

Procession. Directed by Robert Greene. 4th Row Films / Artemis Rising / Concordia Studio / Impact Partners. 2021.

Pulp Fiction. Directed by Quintin Tarantino. Miramax / Jersey Films / A Band Apart. 1994.

RBG. Directed by Julie Cohen and Betsy West. CNN Films / Storyville Films / Better Than Fiction Productions / Participant. 2018.

Reassemblage: From the Firelight to the Screen. Directed by Trinh T. Minh-ha. Trinh T. Minh-ha. 1983.

The Residents. Executive Produced by Dan Partland. Actual Reality Pictures. 2003.

Rich Hill. Directed by Andrew Droz Palermo and Tracy Droz Tragos. Dinky Pictures. 2014.

Rita Moreno: Just a Girl Who Decided to Go for It. Directed by Mariem Pérez Riera. Act III Productions / Artemis Rising / Maramara Films / WNET. 2021.

Roadrunner: A Film about Anthony Bourdain. Directed by Morgan Neville. CNN Films / Tremolo Productions. 2021.

Roger & Me. Directed by Michael Moore. Dog Eat Dog Productions / Warner Brothers. 1989.

Saturday Night with Connie Chung. CBS News. 1989.

Saving Private Ryan. Directed by Steven Spielberg. Amblin Entertainment / Paramount Pictures / Dreamworks Pictures / Mutual Film Company / Mark Gordon Productions. 1998.

Science Fair. Directed by Darren Foster and Cristina Costantini. National Geographic Documentary Films. 2018.

Senna. Directed by Asif Kapadia. StudioCanal / Working Title Films. 2010.

Sherman's March: A Meditation on the Possibility of Romantic Love in the South during an Era of Nuclear Weapons Proliferation. Directed by Ross McElwee. First Run Features. 1985.

The Sixties. Herzog & Company / Playtone. 2014.

Small Farm Rising. Directed by Ben Stechschulte. Mountain Lake PBS. 2012.

Snakes on a Plane. Directed by David R. Ellis. New Line Cinema / Mutual Film Company / Meradin Zweite Productions / Eyetronics / H2L Media Group. 2006.

Sogobi. Directed by James Benning. James Benning. 2004.

The Song of Ceylon. Directed by Basil Wright. General Post Office Film Unit (UK) / Empire Tea Marketing Board. 1934.

Spellbound. Directed by Jeffrey Blitz. Cinetic Media. 2002.

The Staircase (Soupçons). Directed by Jean-Xavier de Lestrade. Maha Productions. 2018.

Startup.com. Directed by Jehane Noujaim and Chris Hegedus. Noujaim Films / Pennebaker Hegedus Films. 2001.

Steve Jobs: The Man in the Machine. Directed by Alex Gibney. CNN Films / Jigsaw Productions. 2015.

The Story of Fathers and Sons. Directed by Catherine Ryan, Gary Weimberg, and Judith Leonard. Luna Productions. 1999.

The Story of Mothers and Fathers. Directed by Catherine Ryan, Gary Weimberg, and Judith Leonard. Luna Productions. 1997.

Stray. Directed by Elizabeth Lo. Magnolia Pictures. 2020.

Susan Starr. Directed by Hope Ryden and D. A. Pennebaker. Drew Associates. 1962.

Teens Get Real. Directed by Catherine Ryan, Gary Weimberg, and Judith Leonard. Luna Productions. 2000.

Tell Me Who I Am. Directed by Ed Perkins. Lightbox. 2019.

They'll Love Me When I'm Dead. Directed by Morgan Neville. Tremolo Productions / Royal Road Entertainment. 2018.

The Thin Blue Line. Directed by Errol Morris. American Playhouse / Channel 4 Television / Third Floor Productions. 1988.

Three Identical Strangers. Directed by Tim Wardle. RAW TV. 2018.

Tiger King: Murder, Mayhem, and Madness. Directed by Eric Goode and Rebecca Chaiklin. Goode Films / Article 19 Films / Library Films / Netflix. 2020.

Time. Directed by Garrett Bradley. Amazon Studios / Concordia Studio / The New York Times / Outer Piece / Hedgehog Films. 2020.

Titicut Follies. Directed by Frederick Wiseman. Zipporah Films. 1967.

Tower. Directed by Keith Maitlin. Go-Valley / Texas Archive of the Moving Image / Meredith Viera Productions. 2016.

The Trials of Muhammad Ali. Directed by Bill Siegel. Kartemquin Films. 2013.

TV Nation. Series directed by Michael Moore. TriStar Television / BBC / Dog Eat Dog Films. 1994–95.

The Underground Railroad. Directed by Barry Jenkins. Amazon Studios / Big Indie Pictures / PASTEL / Plan B Entertainment. 2021.

Una Película de Policias (A Cop Movie). Directed by Alfonso Ruizpalacios. No Ficción. 2021.

Valhalla: The Legend of Thor. Directed by Fenar Ahmad. Profile Pictures / Nordisk Film / Bacon OSL / Bulldozer Film / Netop Films. 2019.

Yesterday, Today and Tomorrow. NBC News. 1989.

Zoo. Directed by Frederick Wiseman. Zipporah Films. 1993.

Interviews with Author

Chadi Abo, visual effects supervisor, March 4, 2020.
Mark Adler, film music composer, June 2, 2021.
Peter Albrechtsen, sound designer and re-recording mixer, March 9, 2020.
Mark S. Andrew, ACE, film editor, October 21, 2019. (Response to online survey.)
Miram Cutler, film music composer, January 6, 2021.
Jacob Dammas, documentary filmmaker, August 10, 2020.
Nainita Desai, music composer, July 10, 2021.
Feras Fayyad, documentary filmmaker, November 9, 2021.
George Foulgham, re-recording engineer, May 21, 2020.
Steve James, documentary filmmaker, March 13, 2020.
Helen Kearns, ACE, film editor, March 30, 2020.
Tamara Kotevska and Ljubomir Stefanov, documentary filmmakers, July 21, 2020.
Penny Lane, documentary filmmaker, March 27, 2020.
Bing Liu, documentary filimmaker, July 20, 2021.
David Michael Maurer, ACE, film editor, October 22, 2019. (Response to online survey.)
Dan Partland, documentary producer and director, May 6, 2020.
Jason Rosenfield, ACE, film editor, March 23, 2020.
Jim Ruxin, ACE, film editor, October 21, 2019. (Response to online survey.)
J. P. Sniadecki, documentary filmmaker and professor, March 16, 2020.
Jez Spencer, re-recording mixer, May 15, 2020.
Karol Urban, CAS, MPSE, re-recording mixer, June 28, 2020. (Interviewed via email.)
Aaron Wickenden, ACE, film editor, February 21, 2020.
Jonathan Zalben, music composer, May 26, 2021.
Amy Ziering, documentary producer, March 31, 2020.
All interviews conducted via Zoom with email follow-up except where otherwise noted.

Index